Meade, Marion

Eleanor of Aqui-
taine

ELEANOR
of Aquitaine

Desmond Seward

Times
BOOKS

Published by TIMES BOOKS, a division
of Quadrangle/The New York Times Book Co., Inc.
Three Park Avenue, New York, N.Y. 10016.

Published simultaneously in Canada by
Fitzhenry & Whiteside, Ltd., Toronto.

First published in Great Britain in 1978 by Book Club Associates
by Arrangement with David & Charles (Publishers) Limited.

Library of Congress Cataloging in Publication Data

Seward, Desmond, 1935–
  Eleanor of Aquitaine

  Includes index.
  1. Eleanor of Aquitaine, Consort of Henry II, 1122?–
1204. 2. Great Britain—Kings and rulers—Biography.
DA209.E6S45 942.03′1′0924 [B]   78–19611
ISBN 0-8129-0749-3

Manufactured in the United States of America.

Contents

Foreword		7
1	Aquitaine and the Troubadours	11
2	Queen of France	25
3	The Crusader	39
4	The Divorce	55
5	Duchess of Normandy	67
6	Queen of England	77
7	The Angevin Empress	91
8	The Court at Poitiers	105
9	Eleanor's Sons	115
10	Eleanor's Revolt	125
11	The Lost Years	135
12	Queen Mother	149
13	The Regent	163
14	Richard's Return	185
15	Fontevrault	195
16	The Death of Richard	205
17	King John	217
18	The Grandmother of Europe	229
19	The Murder of Arthur	239
20	The End of the Angevin Empire	249
	Select Bibliography	257
	Index	261

For Elisabeth Pollington

Foreword

When Eleanor of Aquitaine died in 1204 her long career had been the most colourful and the stormiest of any English queen consort before or since. No other English king has possessed so formidable or so lavishly gifted a wife as Henry II. In her day the greatest heiress in Europe, she became in turn queen of France and queen of England, and among her sons were Richard the Lion-heart and king John. It is not a vulgar exaggeration to call her the sex symbol of her age, for she was as beautiful as she was regal, and universally admired. Splendid in person, in rank and fortune, and in adventure, when young she was the idealized and adored lady for whom troubadours wrote their songs—and whom disapproving chroniclers compared to Messalina.

At the same time Eleanor's story is a family saga. She was very much the royal matriarch who, if not exactly a Livia, ruthlessly dominated her children and turned them against their father. It seems more than likely that her extreme possessiveness helped to bring out their evil qualities, and it may well have been largely responsible for Richard's homosexuality. She feuded bitterly with at least one daughter-in-law and contributed towards the destruction of her own grandson.

The first 'modern' historian to give Eleanor her due as a politician was bishop Stubbs at the end of the nineteenth century. 'This great lady who deserves to be treated with more honour and respect than she has generally met with', he writes of her. The bishop considers that 'she was a very able woman of great tact and experience, and still greater ambition; a most important adviser whilst she continued to support her husband, a most dangerous enemy when in opposition'.

Undoubtedly the key to Eleanor is her thirst for power. She was not prepared to be a mere transmitter of her inheritance to a husband, son or son-in-law, like every other woman in that masculine age. A great independent ruler in her own right, she lost her power when she married Louis VII of France, and later forfeited even her influence over him because of his dependence on monkish advisers and because she failed to bear him an heir. She retrieved neither power nor influence by her second marriage, despite marrying a man more than a decade younger than herself; when she intrigued against Henry she was imprisoned for fifteen years. She at last regained some power as unofficial regent for her son Richard when he was a prisoner in Germany, and then—when a very old woman—even more as the ally of her son John. She had connived at John's succession, bypassing her young grandson Arthur (who was eventually murdered), because John guaranteed her power. As Shakespeare's principal authority for English history, Holinshed, explained in the sixteenth century, 'Surely, queen Eleanor, the king's mother, was sore against Arthur . . . for that she saw, if he were king, how his mother Constance would look to bear the most rule within the realm of England'.

Shakespeare paints a truly appalling portrait of Eleanor in *King John*. Describing John's arrival in France to fight the French king, he says:

> With him along is come the mother queen,
> An Até, stirring him to blood and strife.

Até was a Greek goddess of discord, of criminal folly. Shakespeare stresses John's dependence on his aged mother's strength and cunning, and shows her scheming against Arthur, so 'That yon green boy shall have no sun to ripe', only too pleased to see him in John's murderous hands. She is called 'a canker'd grandam' and 'a monstrous injurer of heaven and earth', and has 'a sin-conceiving womb'. Indeed Shakespeare's 'Queen Elinor', though only a minor character in the play, is one of his most terrifying women, no less evil than Lady Macbeth.

Yet the Elinor of *King John* is only a caricature of one side of a fascinatingly complex personality. When she was young, men worshipped her, and not merely because of her beauty or rank; when she was old, her children venerated her. She could be generous on a truly regal scale. Emerging at Henry II's death from her long confinement as the all-powerful queen mother, she immediately issued an order for the release of prisoners throughout England because, in her words, 'by her own experience prisons were hateful to men and to be released from them was a most delightful refreshment to the spirit'. She also patronized and cultivated the great abbey of Fontevrault, helping to make it a refuge for battered noblewomen fleeing from brutal husbands.

Nonetheless Eleanor has always been overshadowed by her menfolk. Perhaps it is not altogether surprising, with a husband who murdered archbishop Thomas Becket, a son who was the hero of the crusades, and another son who granted Magna Carta. Moreover any heiress would have been dwarfed by so vast an inheritance as Eleanor's duchy; it was the foundation of the Anglo-French empire of the Plantagenets and the origin of the Hundred Years War. The greatest beauty of her age has dwindled into Henry II's rich old wife—remembered for murdering Fair Rosamund, a crime she never committed—or Shakespeare's Elinor and the virago of popular films and television serials. Her loveliness and glamour, her patronage of poets, her throwing-off of the constraints with which convention shackled women in the twelfth century, are all forgotten, as are her very real gifts as a politician and a ruler.

Usually it is all but impossible to write a flesh and blood biography of any figure from the high Middle Ages, expecially a woman, because of the lack of sources. But Eleanor so impressed her contemporaries that there is an abundance of material. This book is an attempt to do justice to a magnificent woman and a magnificent life.

I particularly wish to thank Elisabeth, Viscountess Pollington for reading the typescript and for many useful suggestions. I am also grateful to Mr D.N. Steward and to the Reverend Geoffrey Webb, who gave me valuable advice on certain aspects of the period—the former on the troubadours, and the latter on the abbey and order of Fontevrault. I must thank too Mr Christopher Manning, who read the proofs.

As always I am indebted to Mr Richard Bancroft of the British Library and his staff for their assistance.

1 *Aquitaine and the Troubadours*

'Aquitaine, abounding in riches of every kind.'
Ralph of Diceto

'Her passions are made of nothing but the
finest parts of pure love.'
Shakespeare, *Antony and Cleopatra*

Eleanor of Aquitaine was born in 1122, either at Bordeaux or at the nearby castle of Belin. She was the daughter of the future William X of Aquitaine and his wife Aénor of Châtellerault, and grand-daughter of the duke of Aquitaine then reigning, William IX.

In the twelfth century, France was a geographical expression rather than a country, divided between several peoples who spoke different languages. As yet the Capetian dynasty had little real power. The king was a titular monarch who ruled scarcely more than the neighbourhood around Paris—the Ile de France (so-called because it was almost surrounded by rivers)—together with the Orleannais and Bourges. He enjoyed considerable prestige and moral authority, but he was still no more than the first among many great nobles; although they were his vassals, they nevertheless ruled vast territories as independent princes. The duchy of Aquitaine was the largest of these fiefs. It had passed by inheritance to the counts of Poitiers, and the count-dukes ruled almost the whole of south-western France from the river Loire to the Pyrenees.

Aquitaine proper—roughly the *ancien régime* provinces of Guienne and Gascony—had all the ingredients of a separate nation, and was no less of a country than Brittany. Geographically it was unified by the winding river Garonne and its tributaries, and by such natural frontiers as the Atlantic, the Pyrenees and part of the Massif Central. It possessed racial unity, its people being basically Latinized Basques who had little in common with the Northern French, and its own distinct temperament, which was—and still is—an explosive compound of vivacity and pride. Moreover, it was not merely self-supporting but enviably rich. 'Aquitaine, abounding in riches of every kind', Ralph of Diceto called it, and another chronicler speaks of 'opulent Aquitaine'. From its capital, Bordeaux, wine merchants sailed to England, Germany and Scotland, and from Bayonne men went out to hunt the whale. It was a country of many landscapes, the heaths and sandy wastes of Gascony and the mountains contrasting with flat, lush plains and impenetrable woodland. There were yellow-walled and red-roofed towns, Romanesque cathedrals and rich abbeys. There were also many lordly castles, which were much more comfortable than the chilly keeps of the north, for in the south the tradition of the Gallo-Roman villa had never quite died out.

To the north of Aquitaine was the county of Poitou. Besides its capital of Poitiers, it contained other almost equally fine towns, and La Rochelle was nearly as prosperous a port as Bordeaux. The countryside was an attractive mixture of oak *bocage*, flat farmland—the *plat pays*—and deep pine forest. The Poitevins spoke a dialect of northern French, which to some extent separated them from the Aquitainians.

For the people of Aquitaine, including its rulers and Eleanor herself, spoke a tongue very different from that of Northern France. All the southern French used a number of dialects nowadays known collectively as Provençal, or *langue d'oc*, as opposed to the *langue d'oïl* of the north. One of these dialects, the *Lemosin*, became a written literary language. It was the remarkable achievement of Provençal to create the first vernacular lyric poetry of any merit—with the exception of Irish—in Western Europe since classical times. 'Twelfth century Provençal, softer than sleep', Helen Waddell says of it. She adds that 'Provençal poetry demands no other intellectual background than that of its century, a May morning, the far-off singing of birds, a hawthorn tree in blossom, a crusade for the holy sepulchre. It is the Middle Ages in the medium of a dream'.

The poems of the troubadours were written as songs with lute accompaniment. They might tell of war, politics or rivals, or they could be satirical—as in the form known as the *sirventès*—but usually they were about ladies. A new and widespread devotion to the Virgin Mary had induced something of a reverence for women in general. The troubadours developed a cult of platonic love (*amor de lonh*, love from afar) and sang of an impossible passion for some unattainable noblewoman, invariably married and a great lady, declaiming how lovely she was and how despite her scorn they would continue to adore her. Women of rank— young or even not so young—were surrounded by retinues of sighing troubadours, mostly impoverished petty nobles. In theory, at any rate, physical love played a very small part; a troubadour was expected to think himself well rewarded for ten years of devotion by the gift of a single rose, though he would drop heavy hints for largesse.

This idealization of women, however artificial or exaggerated, brought about a considerable improvement in their status. Whereas in the barbarous north ladies were all too often little more than mere child-bearers, kept in strict seclusion and beaten by their husbands as a matter of course, in the south they enjoyed genuine liberty and mixed freely with the other sex. They were even educated and taught to read, if not to write. The personality of Eleanor—or Aliénor, as she called herself—clearly owed much to the unusually civilized atmosphere of Aquitaine.

The earliest troubadour known by name is Eleanor's grandfather, the fascinating William IX, *Guilhem lo trobador*, who ruled Aquitaine and Poitou from 1086 to 1127. He was the outstanding figure of her early childhood, the first truly big man in her life, and a hero who must have made an enormous impression upon her, even though he died when she was only five. He was a man of extraordinary complexity, alternately idealistic and cynical, ruthless but impractical. He was no statesman and, though aggressive and pugnacious, a notably incompetent general. He failed in one scheme after another. He claimed Toulouse as his wife's inheritance, invading it while its count was away on a crusade, but the invasion ended in disaster and humiliation. In 1101 he himself took an army to the Holy Land; it was cut to pieces near Heraclea and he escaped with difficulty—he may even have spent some time as a prisoner of the Saracens. In 1114 he made another attempt on Toulouse, occupying the county for several years, but he was eventually driven out. In 1119 he went on an expedition to Aragon, helping its king to defeat a multitude of Moors but receiving little reward. He was always in trouble with the Church, and once threatened a bishop with his sword. His private life made a scandalous contrast with his ideals as a troubadour. His most lurid affair was with the dauntingly named Dangerosa of Châtellerault, whom he carried off from her husband, seduced, and then kept in the Maubergeon tower of his palace at Poitiers (from whence she became known as *La Maubergeonne*); and his son rose up in arms at such an insult to his mother. William IX died excommunicated in 1127. For all his talents and his energy, none of his ambitious plans had succeeded. Nevertheless contemporaries undoubtedly respected him as a mighty prince and a brave knight. He successfully cowed and kept in subjection some of the most turbulent vassals in France and he was able to bequeath an undiminished inheritance. Furthermore, even a hostile critic of his own time had to admit that the duke was one of the most courteous people in the world.

Both his age and posterity have been baffled by William IX. First there is his unexpected gift of versifying, in a mixture of Lemosin and Poitevin. He may have been inspired by Arab songs; his father had fought in Spain and brought back Moorish slave girls, and William himself knew Syria as well as Spain. Whatever his inspiration, he was unquestionably a most competent poet, eleven of whose pieces have survived; some are unashamedly licentious, although one, *Pos de chantar m'es pres talenz*, pays a melancholy farewell to earthly joys:

> Since now I have a mind to sing
> I'll make a song of that which saddens me,
> That no more in Poitou or Limousin,
> Shall I love's servant be. . . .

But the originality of a great lord turning troubadour was accompanied by less admirable eccentricities. In one of the earliest known examples of heraldry he had his concubine Dangerosa's likeness painted on his shield, explaining repeatedly that he wanted her over him in battle just as he was over her in bed. He announced his intention of building a special whore house for his convenience, just outside Niort, in the shape of a small nunnery. His frivolity, his satirical wit and his cynicism disturbed contemporaries. 'Brave and gallant but too much of a jester, behaving like some comedian with joke upon joke', Orderic Vitalis says of him, and Orderic is supported by William of Malmesbury, who speaks of the duke as a giddy, unsettled kind of man 'finding pleasure only in one nonsense after another, listening to jests with his mouth wide open in a constant guffaw'. Although never a clown herself, Eleanor took after this grandfather in her sarcastic wit and in the frivolity of her early years.

There was an uncomfortable legend about William IX that Eleanor seems to have remembered. A holy hermit came to him, protesting in God's name at the rape of Dangerosa. He was received with the duke's usual mocking banter. The hermit thereupon laid a curse on William; neither he nor his descendants, whether through the male or the female line, would ever know happiness in their children. When Eleanor was old, bishop Hugh of Lincoln (St Hugh) often told this story, saying that he had heard it from her husband, Henry II, and the king must have heard it from Eleanor herself.

Duke William X, Eleanor's father, was almost as cultured as William IX, just as colourful and still more pugnacious. He was a patron of poets and there were many troubadours at his court, including foreigners from Aragon, Castile and Navarre, and from Italy, and there was even a Welshman called Bledhri. When this duke died, his Gascon friend Cercamon wrote a lament that mourned his passing and the end of his munificence. However, William X was better known for quarrelling than for verses. A man of huge physique and enormous strength, he was an outsize personality in every way. He was said to eat enough for eight ordinary mortals at each meal. He was unwise enough to involve himself in the Church schism that began in 1130, supporting the anti-pope Anacletus against Innocent II; he menaced prelates and ignored excommunications and interdicts that stopped the bells ringing in entire dioceses. He was completely undaunted by the threats of divine punishment that issued from the redoubtable abbot of Clairvaux, St Bernard, and refused to remove a schismatic bishop. When Bernard deliberately entered his territory and publicly celebrated mass at Parthenay, the duke burst into the church in full armour, to teach the infuriating monk a lesson. However, William had met his match. Bernard advanced on him, holding up the consecrated Host, and spoke to such effect that the duke fell to the ground rigid with fear and foaming at the mouth. But although he had lost his battle with the Church, William in no way abated his quarrelsomeness when dealing with his vassals; only his death prevented the whole of the Limousin from rising in revolt.

Very little is known of Eleanor's mother, Aénor. She was the daughter of the viscount of Châtellerault and his wife Dangerosa—William's IX's concubine, the *Maubergeonne*. Aénor had three children: William Aigret (who died when still a boy), Eleanor of Aquitaine and Petronilla (who is sometimes called Aélith). There is a whimsical legend that the name Eleanor—in Provençal, *Aliénor*—is derived from the Latin pun *Alia Aénor*', i.e. 'Another Aénor'. The duchess Aénor appears to have obtained the appointment of her uncle as bishop of Poitiers, perhaps because he was a supporter of Anacletus, and she was probably excommunicated with her husband as an adherent of the anti-pope. The one other detail to survive is that she died at Talmont, about the year 1130, when Eleanor was only eight years old.

William X seems to have been noticeably fond of his eldest

daughter, making her his constant companion. In consequence, Eleanor's childhood was passed under many roofs. Like all rulers of the high Middle Ages, her father was perpetually on progress—administering justice and bringing rebellious vassals to heel—and Eleanor went with him. Inside the Roman city walls of Bordeaux she lived in the Ombrière palace with its tall keep, the 'Crossbowman', although she must also have stayed at the rambling old Tutelle palace just outside. When at Poitiers she inhabited the splendid Maubergeon Tower, which had once housed her grandfather's ladies. There were similar keeps and palaces at Limoges, Niort, St Jean d'Angély, Blaye, Melle, Bayonne and other towns, together with all the fortresses of the vassals. In addition there were many rich abbeys that frequently had the expensive honour of entertaining the ducal household. There were also particularly favoured residences belonging to the duke, such as Belin (near Bordeaux) and Talmont, a castle and hunting lodge on the coast of Poitou.

Eleanor's education was by no means confined to needlework. She was taught to read Latin: first, the prayers and services of the Church, then the Bible, the writings of the fathers and Ovid. She learned to such effect that later she was able to enjoy Latin comedies when they were performed before the court, and it is likely that she could speak the language. She was certainly able to write it—a rare accomplishment for a member of the laity. She was also taught to read and write Provençal, acquiring an expert knowledge of the *gai saber* (joyous art), as the troubadours termed their craft.

Eleanor may well have picked up more than *gai saber* from the troubadours. Many came from the county of Toulouse, which (especially the town of Albi) was the centre of a new religion, a form of Manichaeism. The romantic history of the Albigensians has obsured the nature of their beliefs; they held all matter to be evil, procreation being the ultimate sin. But such views intrigued poets who practised platonic love. Moreover the integrity of the

Albigensian ministers contrasted favourably with the corruption and sloth of all too many of the Christian clergy. Whole districts of southern Aquitaine became Albigensian. Although not even the chroniclers accuse Eleanor of being an Albigensian, there must have been plenty of them at her father's court and it is impossible that she did not know a good deal about their creed.

Obviously Eleanor matured early, partly from being constantly in her father's company. One may guess how much she regretted not having been born a boy and how this regret, together with the freedom bestowed by her position and by Aquitainian court life, made her determined to do just what she pleased and careless of convention. Nevertheless, although she was independent and strong-willed, she was much too feminine ever to be a tomboy; but later she was credited with wearing armour like a man, and she may have displayed a certain casualness in sexual matters.

By this date the Capetian monarchy was at last beginning to assert itself and think of expansion. Louis VI was accused, with justice, of making a god out of his belly, and by his mid-forties he was too fat to mount a horse, yet for all his gluttony he was determined to be more than just 'duke of the Ile de France'. After enforcing strict law and order for the first time throughout the Capetian domains, by military skill and sheer force of character, he then made even his greatest vassals defer to him as a judge and arbitrator, as in the disputed succession to the lordship of Bourbon. By 1124 his vassals had grown dutiful enough to help him fight off an invasion by the emperor Henry V and the English king Henry I. Louis also found other sources of support by issuing to town communes throughout France (though seldom in his own territory) charters to set up corporations, which freed them from feudal obligations to their local lord. Understandably, *Louis le gros* cast greedy eyes on Aquitaine and its heiress. With such a king, Eleanor would have to give priority to a Capetian suitor. In any case, should her father die, the ward-ship of herself and of her fief would fall to the king.

On Good Friday 1137, despite his strength, duke William X died at Compostella, where he had gone to pray to St James the Apostle, and was buried under the high altar at Compostella. Eleanor had no other course than to turn to king Louis. Although a woman could inherit a fief, receive homage from its vassals, and lead them to war, it was also true that under feudal law any ruthless suitor might seize her, force her to marry him, and enjoy her inheritance. It is not known whether William had expressed any wish that his daughter should marry Louis's son but it is more than likely that he had recognized Louis's right to be her guardian. Eleanor was speedily betrothed to *Louis le jeune*, who was Louis VI's only surviving son. Even before the marriage, the fat monarch made his son formally claim Poitiers and Aquitaine and receive the homage of his new vassals at Limoges on 29 June 1137.

The future Louis VII was now sixteen. Originally he had been destined for the cloister and had spent his early years as a 'child monk' at the monastery of Saint-Denis under the benevolent eye of abbot Suger. However, when he was nine his elder brother Philip's horse had been frightened by a runaway pig, giving its rider a fatal fall, whereupon Louis became heir to the throne and was crowned joint-king according to Capetian custom (to ensure an undisputed succession). But the memory of his pious childhood and his affection for monks never left him; he continued his sacred studies and sometimes wore a coarse grey gown and sandals like a simple brother. In appearance he was well built, but not overweight like his father, with long yellow hair and mild blue eyes. His strangest characteristic was his humble, unworldly manner, which none the less gave him a naive charm. Yet he was more intelligent than he seemed at first, and far from ineffectual. His worst faults were an appallingly violent temper—his rages were terrible—and a paralysing sense of sin and guilt.

Louis took over a month travelling from Paris to his wedding, riding by night to escape the heat. He was accompanied by his old friend abbot Suger, who was also his father's trusted minister, by the bishop of Chartres and other prelates, and by an imposing escort of great vassals that included count Thibault of Champagne and count Raoul of Vermandois (a pair of whom Eleanor would later hear a good deal). Naturally he brought sumptuous presents.

Even the monkish young king must have been dazzled by his lavishly gifted bride, when at last he met her. Quite apart from her great possessions, Eleanor was very desirable in herself. So far as one may judge from the contemporary sources and the ecstasies of even the most grudging clerical witnesses, at fifteen she was a beauty—tall, with a superb figure that she kept into old age, lustrous eyes and fine features. (It is likely that her hair was yellow and her eyes blue, as at that time these were considered indispensable for truly remarkable good looks.) Obviously she had inherited the splendid constitution of her father and grandfather. In manner, as befitted a lady who claimed descent from Charlemagne, she was gracious and regal. She must have been far more adult than her bridegroom. Even then she was probably already a protector of troubadours, especially of those fleeing from the irritation of their adored ones' menfolk. (She was to be no less noted for sympathy with her own sex in trouble; her concern for wives who had run away from brutal husbands was later evident in her patronage of the abbey of Fontevrault, which served as a refuge for them.) She was indeed a girl of extraordinary promise.

On Sunday 25 July 1137 the couple were married in the cathedral of Saint André at Bordeaux, by archbishop Geoffrey of Loroux, in the presence of the lords spiritual and temporal of Gascony, Poitou and the Saintonge. Afterwards, at the nuptial banquet in the Ombrière palace, Louis wore the ducal coronet of Aquitaine. Then they went on progress, the wedding night being spent at the castle of Taillebourg.

A fortnight later another ceremony took place in the cathedral at Poitiers. On 8 August Eleanor and Louis were consecrated duke and duchess of Aquitaine with a sacramental rite modelled on that of the service for crowning a king of France. During the banquet in the Maubergeon that followed, abbot Suger brought them the news that Louis VI had died a week earlier, killed by gluttony. For the next fifteen years Eleanor was to see little of Aquitaine.

2 Queen of France

'Les prêtres ne pourraient souffrir aux sacrifices
L'audace d'une femme.'

Racine, *Athalie*

'To live with a woman without danger is more
difficult than raising the dead to life.'

St Bernard, *Sermons on the Canticles*

On Christmas Day 1137, Eleanor of Aquitaine was crowned queen of France at Bourges. Louis also received the sacrament although he had already been crowned. He was infatuated with his beautiful wife, who returned his affection, being only too thankful to be safe from importunate and ruthless suitors. To begin with the couple showed no signs of incompatibility, and for the next few years Eleanor gave herself up to the enjoyment of a court that she made the gayest and most splendid in western Christendom.

Paris, which was to be her principal home, was largely un-walled and unpaved, and many of the ruins of the old Roman city were still standing. Its heart was the walled Ile Saint Louis in the middle of the river Seine, where three centuries before the in-habitants had taken refuge from the Vikings, and which was dominated by the palaces of the king (the *cité* palace) and of the bishop (where Notre Dame now stands). On the right bank the bridge over the Seine was defended by the *Grand Châtelet* (great castle) and on the left by the *Petit Châtelet* (little castle). On the left bank stood the ancient Roman palace of the *Thermae* (baths), a vast rambling edifice whose massive but crumbling masonry had been patched up over the centuries by Merov-ingians, Carolingians and Capetians in their turn, like so many of the city's buildings. On the north bank a growing community of tradesmen, merchants, artisans and money changers had es-tablished itself in a semi-rural area covered by vines, orchards, market gardens and even small farms. Paris was far from being the glorious Gothic capital that it became in the following cen-tury, and as yet was probably no more impressive than the queen's own cities of Poitiers and Bordeaux.

Nevertheless, for so intelligent a woman as Eleanor, Paris and its neighbours must have been extraordinarily stimulating. 'Paris, queen among cities, moon among stars, so gracious a val-ley, an island of royal palaces', wrote Guido of Bezoches in an often quoted passage, 'and on that island hath philosophy her

27

royal and ancient seat: who alone, with study her sole comrade, holding the eternal citadel of light and immortality, hath set her victorious foot on the withering flower of the fast aging world'. For what has been called the twelfth-century renaissance was at its height. There was not yet a university of Paris, but schools of theology and philosophy had sprung up amid the religious houses of the left bank, attended by students from all over the world (including, at that date, an Englishman called Thomas Becket). Currently they were full of Peter Abelard's 'heresies' about individual judgment; in his letters, Abelard claims that ladies of rank were coming to his lectures. It is likely that the queen knew of his ideas, and she may well have heard him speak. Similar schools existed at Orleans, Chartres and Tours, where there were lectures on Plato and Aristotle, the latter only recently re-discovered by scholars travelling in Moorish Spain. Orleans was a stronghold of humanism. The poetry of antiquity was enjoying a new vogue; men were learning to appreciate Horace, Ovid, Virgil and Martial. The twelfth century was also the classic century of the mediaeval Latin lyric. Moreover the troubadours of southern France were echoed in the north by the *trouvères*, who wrote in the *langue d'oïl*, and composed not only love songs but also the epic *chansons de geste*. As for the visual arts, the invention of the pointed arch was about to launch France on the first and most beautiful wave of Gothic architecture. At the deepest level, there was also a spiritual revolution, expressed in the foundation of new religious orders—Cistercians, Carthusians, Premonstratensians, Fontevrault.

Although the queen had Latin plays performed before the court and filled it with troubadours and trouvères, her amusements were on the whole far from cerebral. She introduced Provençal verse and all the elegancies of Aquitaine, including respect for ladies—much to the scandal of churchmen and, no doubt, of northern husbands. The north was equally scandalized by the southern fashions that came with her—the curled beards and short mantles of the men, and the elaborate head-dresses of the ladies.

Although besotted with his beautiful wife, the young king's excessive piety could not be repressed. Eleanor's often frivolous mind can hardly have relished Louis's monkish behaviour—fasting and other austerities, and taking his place in the choir stalls to sing the office with his spiritual brethren. She may have taken more interest in his studies, as she later showed a knowledge of Aristotelian logic, and knew how to use the syllogism in argument. She may well have enjoyed the learned dissertations and disputations that the king arranged in the palace gardens. At this date Louis shared some of his wife's pleasures too, and he seems to have been fond of hunting and the tournament. Deeply in love, he spent a good deal of his time with her and it is possible that he shared at least a little of her taste for poetry. They toured her duchy together, holding court in the great cities.

In those early days Louis VII was full of energy and self-confidence. His asceticism saved him from his father's greed and girth. He had begun well with a marriage that had trebled his domains, and there was every hope that his reign would be a glorious one. He felt himself a match for any of his vassals, and there was no one abroad to threaten him; Germany was torn by disputes over an imperial election, and England was distracted by the miseries of king Stephen's anarchic rule.

Honourable and straightforward to the point of naivety, Louis was becoming renowned for his courtesy, his kindness and generosity, and his simplicity. Once he lay down to sleep in a wood, guarded by only two knights, and when the count of Champagne chided him for his rashness, he replied 'I can sleep alone in complete safety as I have no enemies'. In later life he showed an attractive unworldliness when talking to the Englishman Walter Map about the wealth of kings. Louis said that the monarchs of the Indies possessed jewels and lions, leopards and elephants; the rulers of Byzantium and Sicily had wonderful silks and precious metals; the German emperor commanded fine soldiers and war horses; and the king of England 'lacks nothing—he has gold and silver, precious stones and silk, men and horses, all of them in abundance'. But as for the king of France, 'We have nothing but bread, wine and contentment'.

Louis has his modern admirers. Professor Fawtier tells us that 'historians have been surprisingly slow to appreciate Louis VII at his true worth; and yet his saintly character strongly reminds us of his great-grandson St Louis', and goes on to claim that he was essentially a realist. But on some occasions Louis was far from being either saintly or realistic. It is true that he continued his father's policy with considerable success, eventually establishing complete and lasting control of the Ile de France; he also carried on the extension of the royal authority throughout France by issuing charters to the towns. Nevertheless, despite all his honesty and genuine benevolence Louis had a savage temper and a curiously unbalanced streak that on occasion affected his judgment disastrously.

Masterful and fiercely energetic, Eleanor soon established almost complete control over her husband. Her first trial of strength when she came to Paris was with her mother-in-law. Adelaide of Savoy did not take to her youthful supplanter and soon retired to the estates in Champagne that had been her dowry. It is a testimony to the fifteen-year-old queen's force of character that the battle was won so quicky. Adelaide consoled herself by marrying the lord of Montmorency and passed into obscurity.

Abbot Suger of Saint-Denis was a different sort of adversary, all the stronger for his disarming kindness. This frail little monk of humble origin, who was both an aesthete and a mystic, had been the friend and counsellor of Louis VI and continued to advise Louis VII. He showed unusual compassion for the poor and their sufferings at the hand of rapacious lords. His influence showed in the king's behaviour: building a hunting lodge at Fontainebleau Louis appropriated a peasant's field by mistake; when he learned the truth, he ordered the manor to be demolished and returned the field. Perhaps from Suger too came Louis's tolerance of Jews. But the abbot was also a gifted statesman, anxious to extend Capetian territory and good government. He regarded Aquitaine as a heaven-sent acquisition and did his best to encourage good relations between the king and queen.

Nevertheless Eleanor managed to take his place, sending Louis on expeditions that can hardly have had Suger's entire blessing. When, in the year after their marriage, the bourgeoisie of Poitiers repudiated all feudal obligations to her and set up a corporation or 'commune', Louis and his knights at once stormed the presumptuous city; he then rounded up the sons and daughters of its leading citizens in the square outside the Maubergeon with the intention of taking them back to Paris as hostages. Their frantic parents sent a message to Suger, begging him to intervene. The abbot came as quickly as he could and, with some difficulty, persuaded the king to release the children. It has been plausibly suggested that this merciful act turned the queen against Suger; she did not like people meddling in affairs that directly concerned her. Louis was far from merciful when, shortly afterwards, he had to deal with certain of her vassals who, led by the lord of Lezay, refused to pay homage and stole some valuable gerfalcons from her hunting lodge at Talmont; he cut off their hands with his own sword. In 1141 the king led an expedition against Toulouse, claiming the county for his wife. He achieved nothing and was soon forced to retreat, but Eleanor, who was obviously delighted, gave him a magnificent present—a vase of crystal mounted in gold and set with rich jewels (which can be seen in the Louvre today).

Nevertheless, Louis still retained his interest in ecclesiastical matters. In May 1140, in Sens cathedral (the cathedral church of the primate of France), the king—together with the papal legate and numerous bishops and clergy—presided over the disputation between St Bernard and Peter Abelard. Bernard, who liked to take his sacred texts literally, was infuriated by Abelard's advocacy of examining the scriptures and the writings of the fathers in the light of reason and by his claim that, because logic and philosophy must inevitably be on the side of truth, a sceptical approach was a virtue. In horrified tones, the saint read to the assembly seventeen carefully chosen passages from Abelard's writings that, out of context, sounded damning; the shocked assembly immediately condemned the author without allowing him to defend himself. Later, however, when Abelard went to Rome and appealed to the pope, he was at once absolved of any heresy. Bernard of Clairvaux was a ruthless enemy, as Eleanor was to discover to her cost.

Ironically, the next unfortunate incident in which Louis was involved began with a Church matter. He insisted on appointing his chancellor Cadurc as archbishop of Bourges, despite the fact that Pierre of Le Châtre had been canonically elected and had even received the *pallium* from the pope. The king refused to allow Pierre to enter Bourges, whereupon Innocent II placed France under an interdict; he also sent Louis a stern letter telling him to stop acting 'like a silly schoolboy'. The king's reaction was to take a solemn oath to keep Cadurc as archbishop. Meanwhile Pierre had taken refuge with count Thibault II of Champagne, with whom Louis was already in conflict.

Eleanor's younger sister Petronilla had eloped with count Raoul of Vermandois, who was the king's cousin and grand seneschal of France. Although Raoul was married and much older, the queen gave Petronilla her complete support. Raoul persuaded his brother the bishop of Noyon and two other prelates to annul his marriage on grounds of consanguinity and then married Petronilla with royal approval. Horrified, St Bernard protested to the pope, who excommunicated the bishop of Noyon and ordered Raoul to return to his first wife. No one took any notice.

The countess of Vermandois took refuge with her uncle, Thibault of Champagne, and begged him to help her. Thibault's territory surrounded the Capetian domains; besides being count of Champagne, he was also count of Brie and count of Blois. His attempts to intervene and his protection of Pierre of Le Châtre infuriated the king who, in 1142, invaded Champagne and laid it waste far and wide. The campaign reached its climax in 1143, when royal troops set fire to the town of Vitry-en-Perthois and over a thousand refugees—mainly women and children—perished when the church was burnt to the ground. (The town has been known as 'Vitry-le-Brulé' ever since.) Louis, who was there, was appalled, but no doubt more by the sacrilege than by the slaughter.

The king now received terrible letters from St Bernard, whose abbey of Clairvaux was in Champagne. He was accused of 'slaying, burning, tearing down churches, driving poor men from their dwelling places, consorting with bandits and robbers', and warned that he was in imminent danger of being punished by a wrathful God. The abbot then visited Louis at Corbeil but the interview ended in one of the king's terrible fits of rage. Even so, Louis was overwhelmed by guilt, and badly shaken by the grim monk.

Bernard of Clairvaux had dominated western Christendom—and French public opinion in particular—for many years. When he joined the new Cistercian order in 1113, it possessed only one monastery; at his death, in 1153, it had nearly 350, and the expansion was almost entirely due to his genius as a publicist. From his tiny cell under a staircase at Clairvaux he continually sent out a stream of letters and pamphlets on almost every secular and spiritual issue of the day. In appearance he was like some Old Testament prophet, very tall and emaciated, with a ghastly pallor and white hair, caused by austerities that had aged him before his time. His voice terrified even the bravest opponent. It was inevitable that Louis would give way in the end, but he held out for a surprisingly long time.

Eleanor realized that Louis must be reconciled with Bernard, even though she herself must have been a little afraid of the alarming abbot. The opportunity came at the dedication of Suger's new abbey church at Saint-Denis on Sunday, 11 June 1144. This was the realization of the amiable Suger's dearest dream, the glorification of God by a tangible beauty. This was the first great Gothic church in France, and made full use of the revolutionary pointed arch and rib vault. It was a treasure house, lit by gem-like stained glass and filled with sacred vessels of precious metals studded with rare jewels; the altar furnishings included a gold cross twenty feet tall, and the reliquary of St Denis was cased entirely in silver. Every noble in the realm had contributed some costly ornament, and one of Louis's presents was the crystal vase that the queen had given to him. The crowd was so dense that it was said that inside the church a man might have walked over their shoulders without touching the ground. Everyone of note was there. Among them—perhaps a little surprisingly—was Bernard; he would not tolerate gold and jewels, or even coloured glass, in his order's bleak churches. King and saint were both deeply moved by the ceremony, and exchanged friendly words.

Bernard's meeting with the queen was less successful. It was inevitable that he should disapprove of her: he would not allow his monks to see even their own mothers or sisters, so fearful was he of feminine charms. In a letter intended for the nuns of his order he referred to the devilish vanity of court ladies in their rich dresses made from 'the toil of worms' (i.e. silk), and deplored the painted faces that they removed at night. He had obviously observed these ladies at close hand with shocked fascination: 'Their arms are weighed down with bracelets, and from their ears dangle pendants containing precious stones. For headdresses they wear kerchiefs of fine linen that they drape around their neck and shoulders, a corner falling over the left arm. This is their wimple, usually fastened to their foreheads by a wreath, band or circlet of carved gold.' He must have unsettled his nuns still further by his description of the ladies walking 'with mincing steps, busts thrust forward, garnished and decorated in a fashion more fitting for temples, pulling trains of rich materials after them to raise clouds of dust'. He speaks of some who are not so much ornamented as laden with gold and silver and jewels and 'everything else that accompanies queenly splendour'. One cannot help suspecting that the last phrase refers to Eleanor herself. Apart from her appearance, there was a good deal else that he detested about the queen: her troubadours for example, and her reputation for luxury and frivolity. She did not come of a family that inspired confidence. Her father and mother had been excommunicated, supporters of an anti-pope; as well as being a scourge of bishops and dying outside the church, her grandfather had been a byword for loose living; and her grandmother was the whore and concubine Dangerosa.

To Eleanor, Bernard must have seemed an horrific figure, a white bird of ill omen. Yet she was not shaken. Bernard grumbled that the queen had more power over Louis than anyone else. Later he accused her of meddling, and told her to stop interfering with matters of state. But she persuaded the king to talk to the abbot and to accept a qualified peace with the pope and the count of Champagne. What seems to have enraged Bernard was the suspicion that Eleanor was telling her husband to make conditions rather than to surrender abjectly. The king agreed to withdraw his troops from Champagne, but only if the interdict was lifted.

The queen was sufficiently impressed by the saint to request his prayers in the matter of her barrenness. Apart from one early miscarriage she had not conceived in all her seven years of marriage. Bernard replied: 'Work for peace in the kingdom and I tell you that God of His great mercy will grant your request.'

Peace did not come at once. The new pope, Celestine II,

refused to lift the interdict and fighting broke out once more. Finally Bernard persuaded Celestine to remove the interdict, but in return Louis had to install Pierre of Le Châtre as archbishop of Bourges. Bernard and Suger then reconciled the king with Thibault of Champagne. The pope eventually recognized the marriage of Petronilla and Raoul of Vermandois. Eleanor must take a good deal of the blame for this war.

As Bernard had promised, the queen gave birth to a child as soon as there was peace. Unfortunately it was a girl. She was christened Marie and was one day to marry Thibault's heir and become countess of Champagne.

About this time there occurred the first suggestion of incompatibility between Eleanor and her husband. Although chroniclers and popular historians have accused her of promiscuity, even comparing her to Messalina, nowadays few serious authorities believe that she was physically unfaithful to Louis. On the other hand it is more than likely that she enjoyed flirting. Moreover her frivolity and luxury, her taste for romantic poets, her amusing (and probably frequently erotic) conversation and her sympathy for lovers—e.g. during her sister's elopement—understandably aroused suspicion in monastic minds. The puritanical king himself may well have suspected her, as in the Marcabru affair. The queen had invited this famous Gascon troubadour to Paris; a pupil of her father's favourite Cercamon, his verses were sung and admired throughout the Provençal-speaking world. Marcabru immediately developed the obligatory platonic passion for his beautiful patron, expressing it in songs that were sung everywhere. King Louis took violent exception and angrily banished the all too eloquent poet. (Ironically, most of Marcabru's other poems show a marked contempt for women.)

With hindsight one can see that Eleanor's marriage, which had begun so well, was now threatened from many directions. Louis had suffered a severe nervous crisis during the Champagne war and it is likely that in some way he blamed his wife. She had made a most dangerous enemy in St Bernard, who regarded her as an unsuitable consort for a Christian king. And she had failed to produce an heir to the throne, the first duty of every queen. However, Louis still seemed besotted with her.

3 The Crusader

'Dans l'Orient désert quel devint mon ennui!'
Racine, *Bérénice*

'Debates already 'twixt his wife and him
Thicken and run to head; she, as 'tis said,
Slightens his love and he abandons hers.'
Ford, *'Tis Pity She's a Whore*

On Christmas Eve 1144, Edessa (the capital of a Latin county on the far side of the Euphrates) fell to the Saracens. Christendom was appalled; it seemed that the Holy Land, won back at so much cost only a generation before, might again be lost. After much thought the new pope, Eugenius III, decided that the only way to save it was by a second crusade. In December 1145 he sent a bull to Louis VII, calling upon the king and his vassals to launch an expedition with every resource at their command; in return they would receive forgiveness for all their sins. Later the pope sent a similar bull to the emperor in Germany, Conrad III.

Louis was delighted by the idea. No doubt he sincerely believed that every Christian had a duty to save the land of Christ and His mother from the infidel; and he continued to feel guilty about the holocaust at Vitry, which still had to be expiated by a suitable penance. Eleanor was equally enthusiastic; not only did the prospect appeal to her vigorous and imaginative spirit, but it would provide the change of scene that might well save her threatened marriage, and might even bring down a blessing to end her barrenness. However, Louis's vassals, assembled at Bourges during Christmas, were lukewarm in their response. No king in Christendom—or at least in western Europe— had ever gone to Syria before; and although the First Crusade had been successful, thousands of those who had taken part had perished. Abbot Suger spoke out publicly against the project, expressing his alarm at the thought of the king being so long out of his kingdom. It was a long time before Louis was able to muster sufficient support.

Pope Eugenius therefore turned to his fellow Cistercian, St Bernard, and with Louis begged the eloquent abbot to preach a crusade. The king summoned another assembly to meet at Easter 1146 at Vézélay in Burgundy so that Bernard could appeal to them. It was the last day of March but the weather seems to have been fine. The beautiful Romanesque basilica (for which the town is still famous) was too small to hold the vast multitude that had gathered, so the abbot addressed them from a high make-shift pulpit in the fields nearby. His sermon has not survived, but his burning eloquence had a magical effect. Soon his hearers were shouting 'crosses, give us crosses!' So many wished to sew them onto their clothes in token of their vow that they quickly used up every bit of white cloth available and Bernard had to sacrifice his own white Cistercian choir mantle. Not only the great vassals joined their king in taking the vow, but simple folk in vast numbers also swore an oath to go on crusade. The abbot reported without false modesty to pope Eugenius: 'You ordered and I obeyed; the authority of him who gave the order makes fruitful my obedience; I opened my mouth and I spoke and the crusaders at once multiplied into infinity. Villages and towns are deserted and you will scarcely find one man for every seven women. Everywhere you will see widows whose husbands are still alive.' Bernard then went to Germany, where at Speier, just after Christmas, he shamed the unwilling emperor Conrad into taking the cross.

One woman who was not among the widows made by the abbot's eloquence was Eleanor. She vowed to go to the Holy Land and to pray at Christ's sepulchre in Jerusalem. After all, princesses had accompanied their husbands on the First Crusade: Ida of Austria was believed to have ended her life in a harem. Eleanor had personally sworn on her knees to Bernard that she would bring her vassals, a summons that was her prerogative alone in feudal law, and it would have been impossible to stop her. In any case Louis would not leave her behind; William of Newburgh tells us that he was too jealous of his beautiful wife to do so. She was joined by other great ladies including the countess of Flanders, Torqueri of Bouillon, Faydide of Toulouse and Florine of Burgundy. Indeed William of Newburgh grumbles at the number of female crusaders, and one may suspect that their motives were not always entirely spiritual; tales of the fabulous luxuries of Outremer (as the French then called

Syria and Palestine) were alluring. But not even the chroniclers question Eleanor's sincerity.

The next months were spent preparing for the expedition. A heavy tax was imposed throughout France to raise funds, causing much hardship. Eleanor's officials mulcted her domains with particular ferocity. She herself was busy summoning her chivalry, and among those who promised to come were the lords of Lusignan, Thouars and Taillebourg. Troubadours also responded to her summons, including Jaufré Rudel, who was not to return, and Marcabru, who wrote some crusader songs. The queen made provision for her soul in case she should not come back, endowing abbeys and convents so that they would pray for her—the first evidence of orthodox religious sentiment on her part. Among these was Fontevrault.

The preparations took over a year. Louis appointed Suger as his regent, an inspired choice: the abbot kept excellent order and re-organized the royal finances without increasing the burden on the poor. The king held a final assembly at Etampes in February 1147, debating such matters as the route that the crusaders should take. The lords who attended this council included the counts of Flanders, Toulouse, Dreux and Nevers, the lord of Bourbon and the heir of Thibault of Champagne. In the spring pope Eugenius came to speed the French on their way, meeting the king at Dijon in April. Finally Louis took the oriflamme— the red banner made from St Denis's cloak, which was unfurled only against the enemies of Christ and of France—and after receiving the pope's personal blessing left Saint-Denis on 8 June. Eleanor rode with him.

The French army had assembled at Metz and, having been joined by the king and queen, marched by way of Bavaria and Hungary into the Balkans. The author of the *Gestes de Louis VII*, who was there, writes: 'Anyone watching this multitude of knights, with their shields and helmets gleaming in the sun and their banners waving in the breeze, must surely have believed that they were going to subdue every enemy of the cross and conquer the lands of all the east.' But it was an army of waggons and camp-followers as well as of soldiers, laden with baggage and provisions. The queen and her ladies proved to be an encumbrance, even to the point of demoralization. They had brought with them a horde of maidservants who were an irresistable temptation to the troops: chroniclers grumble at the licence and lechery of the French encampments. Eleanor obviously made her presence felt, to judge from the Greek chronicler Nicetas Choniates, who seems to refer to her when describing women in the French army, 'clad as men, riding horses and armed with spears and battle-axes, and who looked like soldiers, as fierce as Amazons'. He says that at their head rode one to whom he gives the strange title 'lady of the golden boot'. There are similar tales of Amazon-like activities on Eleanor's part to be found in popular western histories—she is even said to have jousted with her ladies—and although they are almost certainly untrue, they do give some idea of her panache.

Eleanor must have had an anxious and far from comfortable journey through the Balkans. The emperor Conrad and his German crusaders had travelled the same road only a few weeks before; their ravaging and plundering had made the population extremely hostile, and food was in very short supply. Nevertheless, the French kept good discipline and, crossing the Danube at Branitchevo, proceeded to Adrianople and thence to Constantinople, which they reached almost without incident on 4 October.

Eleanor and Louis were first installed at the Blachernae Palace on the shore of the Bosphorus, the principal imperial residence, although later they were moved to the Philopatium just outside the city walls. The emperor Manuel Comnenus exchanged the kiss of peace with the French king. According to the latter's chaplain, Odo of Deuil, who was present, they seemed like brothers, as they were about the same age and the same height; but one may guess that the Greek in his purple and gold made a strange contrast to the Frenchman in his grey pilgrim's habit. The crusaders were dazzled by the splendour of the imperial palace: the throne of gold, the columns coated with gold and silver, the pavements of precious marble and the gleaming mosaic pictures. They must have been still more astonished by the ceremonial banquet that followed Manuel's welcome. They tasted for the first time such delicacies as caviar, and they must have been amazed by the profusion of sauces made with rarities such as sugar, pepper and cinnamon. Above all they had to use such unfamiliar implements as wine glasses and forks. The days that followed were spent in similar banquets, in tours of the fabled city and its palaces and churches and in hunting expeditions on which the Greeks employed tame leopards. The markets, with Chinese and Indian silks, Arabian oils and perfumes, Persian carpets, Russian furs, and every other luxury then known, were overwhelming. Manuel and his lords personally conducted the French leader. Some time was spent in haggling about the future of any likely crusader conquests, but Louis was too charmed not to agree to hand over any former Byzantine territories that he might capture.

The Greek emperor was carefully attentive towards Eleanor, who was also fêted by the empress Irene. The latter was a German lady originally called Bertha of Sulzbach, noted for her boast that she stemmed from 'an unconquerably warlike breed'; one suspects that Irene was something of a frump. It must have been a humiliation for the French queen to meet with a refinement of manners and elegance that were beyond her dreams; for this was a city where the material civilization of ancient Greece and Rome had never come to an end, where there was still scientific medicine, plumbing and drainage, and central heating, and where ladies had never ceased using cosmetics. Eleanor acquired a taste for Byzantine clothes and it was probably she who brought back to France such fashions as bulbous turbans, tall pointed hats, and shoes like the beaks of birds.

Despite his amiable reception, Manuel wanted to be rid of his French guests as quickly as possible. He genuinely liked westerners, even if they sometimes attacked his empire. But he could hardly be expected to welcome rapacious troops who terrorized his subjects and upset relations with his Turkish neighbours—relations that depended on a complex and subtly balanced diplomacy. He was therefore pleased to be able to tell Louis that he had just heard of a glorious victory won by the emperor Conrad, in which many thousands of Turks had fallen. Anxious to share in his fellow crusader's triumph, the king left Constantinople after three weeks, no doubt much to Eleanor's regret. The French army crossed the Bosphorus, camping at Chalcedon before marching on to Nicaea, which they reached in early November.

Frightening news awaited them. Contrary to Manuel's information, the Germans had suffered a terrible defeat and had been reduced to a tenth of their original strength. The two armies joined forces and, instead of taking the direct route through Cappadocia as they had originally planned, marched down the Anatolian coast inside Byzantine territory and within reach of ports. The French went first, some of them shouting insults at the German remnants who formed the rearguard. Conrad's health had broken down, so he and his lords sailed back from Ephesus to Constantinople, where he was nursed by Manuel himself.

The French crusaders and the Germans whom Conrad had left behind struggled on, their discipline deteriorating in the winter weather. Eleanor and her ladies travelled in horse-drawn litters whose curtains probably protected them to some extent, but they must have been miserably uncomfortable. On Christmas Day, which was being spent at Decervium, a combination of rain and floods destroyed their tents and baggage and killed many men and horses. Shortly afterwards they began to be attacked by Saracens—Turkish bowmen on fast ponies, who shot from the saddle before closing in with *yataghans* (short sabres). At Pisidian Antioch the heavily armoured French and German knights fought their way across the bridge with difficulty. They were now making for Laodicea in the Phrygian mountains, hoping to shorten the distance to Antioch. In January they found themselves in bleak hill country, the Turks watching from the peaks ready to gallop down and pounce on stragglers. Odo of Deuil tells us that 'the road had become so rugged that sometimes the helmets of the knights touched the sky while sometimes their horses' hooves trod the very floor of hell'. Constant harassment by the enemy, winter storms, shortage of food and suspicion of Byzantine guides were breaking down the crusaders' morale.

Near Attalia there was almost a disaster that might have destroyed the entire Christian army. One evening, instead of obeying Louis's orders to camp on the crest of the pass through which they were travelling, the French advance guard went on down into the less exposed valley. (Not at Eleanor's suggestion, as some contemporaries seem to have suspected.) This enabled the Turks to get between it and the main body of the army, which—after seizing the high ground of the pass—they at once attacked. Desperately the knights charged uphill at them but were beaten back in confusion. Louis had his horse killed beneath him and was surrounded by the enemy; he saved himself by climbing onto a rock and, with his back to the mountain, managed to parry the *yataghans* of the exultant Turks until he was rescued. Probably he owed his life to his plain armour, which prevented the enemy from recognizing him. Many of the crusaders were slain, their comrades being saved only by the onset of darkness.

Next day Louis gathered his battered army together and handed over command to a really experienced soldier, the Master of the Knights Templar, whose contingent was the only one that had kept its discipline. The Templars brought what was left of the army safely down to Attalia. It proved to be a poor place without enough food, and the king decided that his only hope of reaching the Holy Land was by sea. He had to spend more than a month hiring ships, during which time the Turks raided the neighbourhood around the town relentlessly. When the fleet was ready, there was no room for the infantry or the pilgrims, so Louis abandoned them to struggle on by land as best they might, and set sail with his chivalry.

It was a dreadful voyage, made terrifying by seasonal storms. Amid the howling wind and the high waves Eleanor may even have wished herself back in her jolting litter being shot at by Turks. To convert them into horse transports, the ships had had great doors cut in their hulls, which were caulked before sailing, and there was a constant danger that they would be stove in. A century later another crusader, Joinville, wrote: 'For what voyager can tell when he goes to sleep at night whether or not he may be lying at the bottom of the sea the next morning?'

After three weeks the storm-tossed fleet eventually reached Saint Symeon, the northernmost port of the Latin principality of Antioch, on 19 March 1148. As they disembarked, the French king and queen were greeted by priests singing the *Te Deum* and by the prince of Antioch and his entire court, who escorted them back to the capital. Their arrival at Antioch was celebrated by tournaments, banquets and pageants. It was the brief but enchanting Syrian spring, with gardens and hillsides a mass of flowers, and the sunlight gentle but clear. Antioch, on a mountain slope above the river Orontes, had eight miles of walls, 360 bastions, and countless villas, palaces, and terrace gardens, and was still almost the glorious city of antiquity.

For the crusaders, Outremer must have been no less dazzling than Constantinople. The Latin settlers dressed like Saracens in silken turban and burnous, their ladies' painted faces veiled against the sun. To a visitor from the primitive west the luxury of their villas seemed sinful; outside there were courtyards, rooftop gardens and fountains and wells with water piped from mighty aqueducts; inside there were mosaic floors, carpets on which to sit, tableware of gold, silver and faience, coffers inlaid with ivory and sandalwood, sunken baths, and beds with sheets. Among the novelties were soap, sugar, spices, fruits—lemons, oranges, pomegranates, persimmons—fabrics such as cotton and muslin, and the miracles of oriental medicine. Obviously the queen enjoyed it all immensely.

During her ten days at Antioch, Eleanor's dangers and hardships were amply recompensed by such entertainments as picnics on the banks of the river Orontes, with delicacies such as snow-cooled wine and gazelle hunts with falcons. Her pleasure must have been increased by meeting many Aquitainians among the leading settlers; even the patriarch came from Limoges. But Eleanor's chief diversion was the prince of Antioch himself, her long-lost uncle Raymond of Poitiers, who was still only in his forties.

Much of Raymond's colourful personality is symbolized by the way in which he acquired his principality. When Bohemond II was slain in battle by the Turks in 1130 his ambitious widow Alice offered to marry her daughter Constance—who was Bohemond's heiress—to a son of the Byzantine emperor. The horrified Latin barons and prelates of Antioch appealed for help to king Fulk of Jerusalem. Fulk decided that Raymond, being of excellent capabilities and ducal birth but landless, would make a suitable prince, and sent secret messengers to him in England at Henry I's court. To avoid being arrested en route by the Sicilian king, who also had designs on Antioch, Raymond travelled to the East in disguise, sometimes as a pedlar, sometimes as a poor pilgrim. When he arrived he revealed himself to Alice and immediately proposed marriage. His proposal was accepted but, while Alice was preparing for her wedding, Raymond—with the connivance of the Latin patriarch—surreptitiously married the nine-year-old princess Constance in the cathedral. He was now ruling prince of Antioch by right and the unfortunate Alice had to depart into obscurity.

Raymond I's ingeniously won principality was a rich and glorious one, but he was constantly threatened by either the Turks or the Greeks and had to spend most of his time on dangerous campaigns or in complicated and hazardous diplomacy. However, he was a brave and resourceful ruler and extremely popular with his Latin, Greek and Saracen subjects.

In addition Raymond was tall and good-looking, with great personal magnetism. Sir Steven Runciman says of him: 'He was handsome and of immense physical strength, not well educated, fond of gambling and impetuous and at the same time indolent, but with a high reputation for gallantry and for purity of conduct.' He could bring a war horse to a halt by the grip of his thighs, and was a famous jouster and huntsman. As befitted the son of William IX, he liked to have poems and chronicles read to him.

Unfortunately the immediate liking that sprang up between uncle and niece was so demonstrative that, despite Raymond's reputation for 'purity of conduct', there were actually whispers of incest. But we hear of this allegation only from a chronicler who wrote forty years later. There are other legends of the queen's immorality that we know to be completely unfounded; she was said to have become infatuated with a Saracen slave, although he was only a boy, and even to have slept with sultan Saladin himself—who at this date was thirteen and whom she certainly never met. Admittedly, Eleanor was quite capable of being unfaithful to a husband as monkish and bloodless as Louis. But reliable contemporary writers such as John of Salisbury and Gervase of Canterbury are plainly convinced of her innocence. There is no evidence that she slept with her uncle, and no serious historian now believes the accusation.

Nonetheless it is undeniable that the king was angered by his wife's affection for prince Raymond. The explanation seems to lie in a disagreement over the purpose of the French crusade.

Raymond wanted to use such a reinforcement to attack the most dangerous Saracen strongholds, in particular Aleppo; he even hoped to reconquer and restore the lost county of Edessa. He had too few troops of his own and without help there was a possibility that he might be overrun by the Saracens; and if Antioch fell, all Outremer would be in danger. But Louis decided to go on to Jerusalem, and clung to his resolve with all the obstinacy of a weak young man. Perhaps he resented the excessive self-assurance of his elegant and possibly patronizing host, and he may have nursed suspicions of Raymond's relations with the Greeks, whom Louis had now grown to hate.

Eleanor was outraged by her husband's stupidity. In front of everyone she spoke long and passionately in favour of her uncle's plan. Infuriated by what must have seemed open contempt for him, the king announced that he was leaving Antioch without further delay and that as a dutiful wife she had to accompany him. The queen, by now equally angry, answered that he might go but she would stay in Antioch, and that furthermore she wanted their marriage annulled on grounds of consanguinity (i.e. that they were within the degree of kinship that made a marriage canonically illegal). One unreliable chronicler claims that she told Louis he wasn't 'worth a bad pear'.

The king's paymaster, a Templar named Thierry Galeran, was a eunuch of whom Eleanor had made an enemy by mocking at his disability. No doubt with relish, Thierry advised Louis to use force. Accordingly in the middle of the next night, royal troops broke into the queen's palace and dragged her off to the St Paul gate, where her husband was waiting. They left Antioch secretly, before dawn.

Louis wrote to Suger complaining about Eleanor, but the wise abbot replied: 'With regard to the queen your wife, I think you should conceal any displeasure until you are back in your own kingdom, when you will be able to consider the matter more calmly.' The king seems to have taken this advice, but the rift between the couple never really mended.

Flaws in Louis VII's character, brought out by the strains of the crusade, may be discerned in his attitude towards the Greeks. He hated them because of their failure to help him in Anatolia, most unjustly blaming his misfortunes on the emperor Manuel. One may even guess at an element of paranoia.

After the French king and queen had at last reached Jerusalem—where Louis was welcomed 'as an angel of the Lord'—and fulfilled their vow to pray at the Holy Sepulchre, they went on to Acre, which was the second city and chief port of the little kingdom. Here they found an imposing assembly that included the young king Baldwin III of Jerusalem and his Palestinian barons together with the emperor Conrad and many German lords. Louis allowed himself to be talked into joining a great and misguided expedition against the hitherto friendly Saracen city of Damascus. It ended in disaster, the Latin army having to beat a humiliating retreat and suffering many casualties. Despite letters from Suger that implored him to come home, however, Louis insisted on staying in the kingdom of Jerusalem for another year. Whatever the quarrel between them, Eleanor can hardly have been averse to such agreeable surroundings. And she had the acid consolation of knowing that if only her husband had taken her advice and co-operated with Raymond of Antioch, Outremer would now have been rejoicing instead of lamenting the *débâcle* at Damascus.

Some time after Easter 1149, Louis and Eleanor at last left the Holy Land, sailing from Acre in separate ships. There was war between Sicily and Byzantium and the queen's vessel was captured by the Greek emperor's ships off the Peloponnese coast. The king's vessel escaped, and when, after an exhausting voyage that lasted several weeks, he landed on the shore of Calabria, he did not know whether his wife was still alive; he shows little emotion in a letter giving Suger the news. King Roger of Sicily was happy to inform him that his navy had recaptured Eleanor's ship and that she had been recuperating at Palermo, where she insisted on staying for at least a fortnight longer.

Anyone so intelligent as Eleanor would have been intrigued by the extraordinary Sicilian court. Its Norman king dressed in robes of Byzantine purple embroidered with kufic lettering and weird animals in gold, worshipped according to the Latin rite in Greek churches, and kept his wife in a harem. His army contained Frankish knights and Saracen infantry, and his government was administered by Norman chamberlains, Byzantine *catapans* and Arab *cadis*. The luxury rivalled that of Constantinople and Antioch. She must have been most reluctant to rejoin her husband on the Italian mainland.

As for Raymond of Antioch, his niece never saw him again. About the time that she was setting sail from Acre, in June 1149, he fell in battle against the Saracens. His skull was set in silver and sent to the caliph of Baghdad.

4 The Divorce

'*Peut-être on t'a conté la fameuse disgrace*
De l'altière Vasthi. . . . .'

Racine, *Esther*

'Let it be known among the laws of the Per-
sians and the Medes, that it be not altered,
that Vashti come no more before King Aha-
suerus; and let the king give her royal estate to
another that is better than she.'

The Book of Esther

The end of Louis and Eleanor's marriage was plainly in sight. The king had been so affected by his experiences during the crusade that he spent even longer hours at prayer, and cropped his head and shaved his beard like a priest. Eleanor's comment was 'I married a monk, not a king'. He no longer slept with her, although, given the mediaeval Christian's distrust of physical love, it is unlikely that he had ever spent much time in her bed. (This is probably the reason why she had borne only one child; later she presented a more virile husband with five sons and three daughters.) Meanwhile they continued their journey homeward by land, having had enough of sea voyages, and rode glumly northward through Italy.

The atmosphere must have been tense with misery. Louis was obsessed by the consanguinity that Eleanor had raised so furiously at Antioch. Even during the Champagne war St Bernard had asked why the king could take such exception to the consanguinity of Raoul of Vermandois and his wife when Louis and Eleanor were themselves related within the fourth, forbidden degree. Moreover, the pope had eventually accepted Raoul's plea and recognized the annulment. As the king always had a most delicate conscience and was a martyr to scruples, he was tormented by guilt. His anguish was made worse by the fact that despite all their quarrels he was still passionately in love with Eleanor.

The unhappy pair reached Tusculum on 9 October 1149. Here the papal court was in residence, having fled from Rome (which was threatened by imperial troops in one of the perennial conflicts between pope and emperor). Eugenius III gave them a warm welcome, as we know from the history of John of Salisbury, then a papal secretary, who was present. Louis took the opportunity to confess his misgivings about the validity of his marriage. The pope told him to ignore them, to forget the very word consanguinity; if necessary, a dispensation could be provided by the Church. John noted that despite his scruples the king loved Eleanor with an almost childish love. He also observed that one of Louis's confidants—presumably Thierry Galeran—was constantly trying to poison his mind against the queen. Eugenius tried hard to reconcile the couple. He forced them to sleep together, personally conducting them to a guest room furnished with splendid silk hangings but with only one bed. This austere pontiff—originally a Cistercian monk—was obviously moved by their predicament. When they left, Eugenius could not keep back his tears as he blessed both them and France.

Eleanor and Louis travelled on to Rome. Here they were taken on a tour of the Eternal City by cardinals whom Eugenius had sent with them for the purpose. They rode on over the Alps, through the Jura, and at last reached Paris in November 1149. They had been away for two years and six months. The regent Suger, who met them at Auxerre, handed back to his master a realm that was as peaceful as it was prosperous.

The royal marriage had not been healed by Eugenius. Suger, who still possessed more influence over Louis than anyone, did his best to save it. He considered the extension of Capetian rule throughout France to be the will of God and dreaded a divorce that would lose the monarchy Aquitaine. In the summer of 1150 Eleanor bore her second child—not an heir, but another daughter (Alice, who would one day be countess of Blois), whose birth did nothing to reconcile her parents. Then, in January 1151, abbot Suger died.

According to an English chronicler, after Louis and Eleanor returned to France they began to quarrel over everything. It was now that she took such offence at his habits and began to grumble again about being married to a monk. Unquestionably Louis was more devout then ever. He made yet another pilgrimage of expiation to Vitry-le-Brulé, planting Cypress trees that he had brought back from the Holy Land (whose descendents still grow there today). He continued to take advice from men who were enemies of the queen, including Thierry Galeran.

For the time being, however, the king was too busy with a feudal dispute to worry about his marriage. He found himself at war with one of the most formidable of French vassals—Geoffrey Plantagenet, count of Anjou. The quarrel was over Geoffrey's treatment of Rigaud Berlai, the lord of Montreuil-Bellay near Saumur. Rigaud was the count's most turbulent vassal, who constantly ravaged his lands. Unfortunately he was also Louis's seneschal in Poitou. When the king left France on crusade the count began a siege of Montreuil-Bellay that was to last for three years. As soon as Louis returned, Rigaud appealed to him for help, but only when Geoffrey finally stormed and burned Montreuil-Bellay, shackling Rigaud like a common felon, did the king intervene. He beseiged Arques in Normandy—where the count's son was duke—and sacked Séez. He was soon made to realize that he was facing dangerous and resourceful opponents. Bernard of Clairvaux stepped in and Geoffrey and Louis agreed to let him arbitrate. Accordingly the count and his son, Henry FitzEmpress, rode to Paris bringing the miserable Rigaud with them, still in chains.

They reached Paris in August 1151. Henry paid homage for his new duchy of Normandy and Louis received it, recognizing him as duke; but there was an unedifying wrangle over Rigaud. Bernard had had the count excommunicated for attacking Rigaud while the king was away on crusade and breaking 'the truce of God'. He graciously offered to absolve Geoffrey if he would release Rigaud at once. To the saint's angry astonishment the count refused, saying that he hoped God would not forgive him if imprisoning Rigaud had been a sin. Bernard prophesied an early and evil end for a man who could utter such blasphemy. Eventually Geoffrey became more reasonable and after his son had agreed to hand over most of the Vexin (on the Norman border) the two sides agreed on a peace settlement.

Eleanor seems to have been very impressed by these two visitors. Geoffrey was a fine-looking man (his other nickname besides Plantagenet was 'the Handsome') and territorially he was almost as powerful as Louis. He had married the lady Matilda, widow of the emperor Henry V and daughter and heiress of Henry I of England: her cousin Stephen of Blois had usurped the throne, but her supporters were many and there was a good chance that her son by Geoffrey would one day become king. Gerald of Wales claims that Geoffrey made adulterous advances to queen Eleanor; but most chroniclers agree with William of Newburgh that she was more attracted by Geoffrey's son, Henry. In the stern words of her Victorian biographer, Miss Strickland, 'Eleanor acted with her usual disgusting levity in the advances she made to this youth'. But William of Newburgh says simply that the queen desired a marriage with the young duke on the grounds of compatibility, which is quite possible. The fact that Henry was eleven years her junior is irrelevant: his father was eleven years younger than his mother Matilda. And by now Louis was growing more and more difficult; Eleanor must daily have anticipated the end of her marriage. Indeed, in the light of what followed, it is more than likely that she reached some sort of secret understanding with Henry.

Nevertheless it is almost certain that during the whole of her marriage she was faithful to Louis. Her reputation may well have suffered from speculation about so beautiful a woman—speculation superficially confirmed by her clothes and by her jokes.

The catalyst that ended her marriage was St Bernard. Sure enough, his curse struck Geoffrey down within a matter of days. The journey back to Anjou was a hot one and on the way the count went for a swim in a little stream that ran into the Loire; the same night he was stricken by a fever and three days later, on 7 September, he died. Everyone must have remembered the saint's prophecy. Now that Suger was dead, Bernard's influence on king Louis was irresistible.

St Bernard is an enigma. The holiness of the 'last of the

fathers of the church' is undeniable. His concept of God was revolutionary in its humanity and tenderness, and he inspired thousands to follow him into one of the most austere forms of community life ever devised. He could be surprisingly kind to those who did not share his views, and condemned the persecution of the Jews. On the other hand he often showed a lack of charity, as in his destruction of Abelard. He was ruthless in implementing what he believed to be God's will, which he interpreted with total assurance. It was almost certainly Bernard who ended Eleanor's marriage.

The saint had never lost his suspicions of Eleanor. The contrast between king and queen was obvious to everyone—the *dévot* Louis surrounded by monks, and the frivolous 'wanton' in the midst of her troubadours. Such a woman was a most unsuitable consort for an annointed monarch with a soul to save. Moreover it was essential for the Capetian monarchy that Louis should have a son and heir who could be crowned joint king to ensure a smooth succession when his father died. Like Suger, Bernard believed that it was God's purpose that the Capetian dynasty should survive and triumph, but unlike Suger, he had no qualms about losing the queen's dowry. Nor, whatever the pope might have said, had he any reservations about manipulating canon law in order to obtain an annulment. In the Middle Ages, annulments were given so freely that they amounted to a tacit system of divorce. As has been seen, consanguinity was a useful pretext.

It was inevitable that Louis would lose Aquitaine if he repudiated his wife. He held it only as Eleanor's consort, and she was extremely popular with its unruly barons, who could be relied on to fight for her against the king of France. He might have accused her of adultery and confiscated her fief, but adultery by a queen was treason and carried the death penalty, and after such an outrage Aquitaine would have been impossible to subdue. Some historians think that the great duchy constituted a

THE CHILDREN OF LOUIS VII (1120-1180)

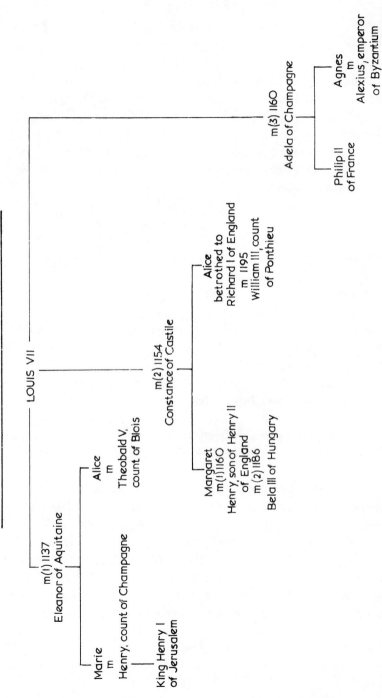

potential millstone around Louis's neck. Professor Fawtier considers that the king had neither the men nor the money to rule it—'The attempt to keep order there would have exhausted the Capetian monarchy, backed only as it was by its incompletely pacified little royal domain'—and that sooner or later Louis would have found himself embroiled in an exhausting war with his wife's vassals. In support of this view it has to be admitted that he ruled the Ile de France only with difficulty and that he does not seem to have received any significant revenue from Aquitaine. On the other hand Louis and the Aquitainians had lived together peacefully since 1137, and to relinquish the duchy might well have added to the power of some hitherto unforeseen enemy—as indeed turned out to be the case. It would be an abdication that could halt the advance of the Capetian monarchy for ever.

Finally Louis decided on an annulment, whatever the risks. One can guess at a long and agonized internal debate, although one may suspect with justice that there was strong pressure from St Bernard. Probably what eventually caused the king to make up his mind was the absence of an heir.

The royal couple's last enterprise together began after the departure from Paris of count Geoffrey and his son. They set out in September on a long progress through Aquitaine, accompanied by an imposing train of bishops and barons that included the archbishop of Bordeaux as well as the unwelcome Thierry Galeran. Christmas was kept at Limoges, and Candlemas at Saint-Jean d'Angély. It is evident that both Eleanor and Louis were anticipating separation in the near future, as throughout the progress French seneschals and castellans were replaced by Aquitainians. Then they returned to the king's territory, to Beaugency.

Here a council of the French clergy had been summoned. It met on 11 March 1152 under the presidency of the archbishop of Sens, primate of France. On 21 March the marriage of king

Louis and queen Eleanor was pronounced null and void on the grounds that they were third cousins. It is said that the annulment was heartily approved by St Bernard, but some chroniclers report that pope Eugenius tried to forbid it. Unreliable sources suggest that the queen was accused of adultery but it is almost certain that this is untrue; the proceedings had obviously been carefully arranged beforehand with the agreement of both parties.

In *Les Annales d'Aquitaine* the seventeenth-century historian Jean Bouchet claims that queen Eleanor was cast off. He describes how she waited in anguish outside the council chamber and collapsed when she heard the verdict, remaining in a faint for two hours, and how when she revived she defended herself in a passionate speech. This moving account is pure invention. It is quite clear that Eleanor was only too anxious for a separation and made no attempt to dispute the annulment, even though she had to give up her two little daughters.

Eleanor quickly left Beaugency for Poitiers. But she was once again a fabulous heiress. At Blois, count Thibault—the son of Louis's old enemy in the Champagne war—was so insistent in his courtship that she had to escape by night, taking a barge down the Loire to Tours. Here she learned that seventeen-year-old Geoffrey of Anjou, a younger brother of duke Henry of Normandy, was lying in ambush for her at the crossing of the little river Creuse at Port-de-Piles, no doubt with the intention of forcing her to marry him. Travelling by a little-used road, however, she at length reached Poitiers and her palace of the Maubergeon.

Eleanor and her favourite son, Richard I. *Archives Photographiques, Paris.*

Eleanor of Aquitaine: the effigy at Fontevrault. *Photo Jean Feuirrie.*

5 Duchess of Normandy

'Now she pays it.
The misery of us, that are born great,
We are forc'd to woo, because none dare woo us.'

Webster, *The Duchess of Malfi*

'. . . the duchess of Normandy, who was young and of great worth and understood courage and honour and liked songs in praise of her. The songs of Bernart [de Ventadour] pleased her and she took him for her guest and made him welcome. He was long at her court and fell in love with her, as she did with him. But while he was there, king Henry of England married her and took her from Normandy and led her away.'

Raynouard, *Choix des poésies originales des troubadours*

Eleanor had escaped from an unhappy and frustrating marriage, but—as was so painfully demonstrated during her journey home—found herself in an even more humiliating situation. This stately and masterful lady, who as queen of France had been accustomed to deference and respect, might now expect as unmarried heiress to Aquitaine to be seized at any moment and married at the point of the sword. She was once more what she had been when her father died—the quarry of every fortune hunter and robber baron.

The only escape possible was remarriage to a man of her own choice. An English chronicler (Gervase of Canterbury) suggests that Eleanor dispatched envoys to Henry, duke of Normandy, to offer him her hand, but this is unlikely. What probably happened was that she sent secretly to Henry accepting an offer that he had made, perhaps in Paris the previous summer. Her vassals had already been summoned to meet her, ostensibly to consider military matters, and she was therefore able to ask for their approval of the match without delay. Ironically, although she was no less closely related to the duke than she was to Louis, the couple did not bother to obtain a papal dispensation (although in 1146 a proposed marriage between Henry and Eleanor's daughter had been vetoed by St Bernard on the grounds of consanguinity). On Whit Sunday, 18 May 1152, eight weeks after the annulment of her first marriage, the duchess of Aquitaine was married to the duke of Normandy in the cathedral church of Saint-Pierre at Poitiers.

After her ex-husband, Henry was unquestionably the most eligible bachelor in France. Besides Normandy he had inherited Maine, Anjou and Touraine from his father and he had a good chance of obtaining England as well. As has been seen, the fact that he was eleven years younger—he had been born in 1133—was no obstacle. In person he was a big stocky man of enormous energy and physical strength, with a deep barrel chest and the bandy legs of a horseman. He had a large round head with a

69

square freckled face, bulging blue-grey eyes, and close-cropped red hair and beard. He was carelessly dressed, blunt and unceremonious in manner and without any trace of his mother's notorious arrogance. He was as energetic and restless as he was moody, constantly on horseback, moving endlessly from place to place. An expression amiable to the point of gentleness could change suddenly and terrifyingly, his face purple and his eyes shot with blood; there were astonishing outbursts when he would roll on the floor screaming and biting the rushes. He ate little and drank even less, his chief amusements being hunting and hawking. He was no less vigorous in mind than in body, and unusually well educated. (Twelfth-century magnates were often surprisingly literate: the duke's father had learnt his military strategy by studying Vegetius's *De re militari*.) Henry read and wrote Latin—which he spoke fluently in his hoarse, cracked voice—as well as French and Provençal, and is said to have had some knowledge of every tongue 'from the coast of France to the river Jordan'. He would frequently withdraw to his chamber with a book. For all his vigour and intelligence, however, Eleanor can scarcely have realized that she was marrying one of the great men of her century.

Eleanor no doubt thought that in marrying a much younger man she was obtaining a biddable husband who would let her keep her newly regained power. She was mistaken; but to begin with, the marriage between the eighteen-year-old duke and the twenty-nine-year-old duchess seems to have been happy enough. Henry was passionately in love with Eleanor's mature beauty and intellect. As highly sexed as he was vigorous—to judge from his string of mistresses—he gave his wife all the children she wanted; and although he preferred scholars to troubadours, he shared at least some of her intellectual pursuits.

Politically, Henry had taken a calculated risk in marrying Eleanor. The effort needed to keep Aquitaine and its aggressive baronage under control might well prove so exhausting as to hamper him in winning England. On the other hand, if she had taken someone else for her husband he would have been a constant threat to Anjou, which was separated from Poitou only by the river Loire. And Henry was never frightened of taking risks.

Louis was horrified by the news. No doubt he had expected any prospective suitor of his former queen to ask his permission before marrying her. After all, Eleanor was his ward and Henry was his vassal, so they were legally bound to seek his leave. It was just the sort of callow misjudgment that Louis would make. Plainly he and his advisers were horrified by the tidings, realizing that they had made a terrible political blunder. Some of the outrage felt by the French court is echoed by the malicious lie recorded by a chronicler that Henry's father, Geoffrey Plantagenet, had been Eleanor's lover and for this reason had forbidden his son to marry her. At one stroke all abbot Suger's worst forebodings had come to pass. Not only had the Capetian monarchy let Aquitaine slip from its fingers but the duchy had been snapped up by one of the king's most formidable vassals. If Henry obtained England in addition, he would be the most powerful ruler in western Christendom.

As usual Louis VII reacted violently and too late. Nevertheless he managed to assemble a dangerous-looking coalition. It included the king's brother, the count of Dreux, whose lands bordered Normandy; the new count of Champagne; Henry's younger brother Geoffrey, whom he had deprived of the four castles left to him by his father and who hoped to become count of Anjou in his place; and Eustace, count of Boulogne, who was king Stephen's eldest son and heir, and Henry's rival in the succession to the English throne. Quite apart from what they might take from the duke's territory, these five intended to conquer Aquitaine and divide it between them. Henry, himself naive on this occasion, had not expected such a storm. He was busy on the Norman coast preparing to invade England when in June he heard that Louis was attacking his eastern borders. He rode to meet him at such a ferocious pace that many of his men's horses foundered, and, when the French king retreated hastily, laid waste Dreux and then struck southward, capturing Geoffrey's chief stronghold of Montsoreau and Geoffrey himself together with most of his supporters. Louis retired to his bed with a fever, worn out after only two months of fighting this alarming opponent, and agreed to a lengthy truce.

Henry and Eleanor then went on progress through her domains. The inhabitants were quickly taught that their new master was a very different man from Louis VII. At Limoges, when the monks of the abbey of Saint-Martial refused feudal dues by a legal quibble, he promptly demolished the walls that had only recently been built to protect both abbey and town. No rebelliousness is recorded elsewhere in Aquitaine at this time.

In January 1153 duke Henry sailed for England, landing in Dorset and making for Bristol, which had always remained loyal to Matilda's cause and from where her party controlled a large area of the southwest, extending as far east as Wallingford on the river Thames. He was soon joined by Robert earl of Leicester and later earl Ferrers came over to him with other former supporters of king Stephen—many English lords had lands in Normandy. In July he relieved the heroically loyal town of Wallingford, while another group of his supporters under Hugh Bigod, earl of Norfolk, also waged an effective campaign. Stephen, brave but incompetent, fought on in the hope that he might be able to bequeath his crown to his eldest son Eustace; he still controlled most of England, and Eustace was ruthless and determined. But in the middle of August, count Eustace choked on an eel during dinner at Bury St Edmunds, where he had been plundering the abbey lands. Stephen was heartbroken. Abandoning the claims of another son, at Christmas at Westminster he formally recognized the duke of Normandy as his heir, and in January 1154 at Oxford he made his barons do homage to Henry as their future king.

While her husband was away in England, Eleanor's principal residence appears to have been Angers, the capital of Anjou. It was—and still is—a most agreeable town on a beautiful site overlooking the river Loire, with fine buildings that included a strong palace-citadel. There were abbeys both inside and outside its walls and even schools of learning as at Orleans and Chartres. The local white wines were already famous.

On 17 August 1153 she gave birth to her first son, who was named William after her father and grandfather. Meanwhile Eleanor was able to amuse herself in a way that had all too often led to trouble when she was married to Louis. No doubt remembering Marcabru, the duchess gave shelter to an even more famous troubadour, Bernart de Ventadour. Despite his lordly name he was not a nobleman; his mother had been a kitchen servant of the family of Ventadour in the Limousin. There was a tradition of *gai saber* in this family and the lords of Ventadour encouraged Bernart to cultivate his remarkable poetic talent. As so often, the young man's verses to the lady Alaiz, wife of Eble II of Ventadour, were a little too warm; the affair ended with Alaiz being imprisoned and then cast off, and Bernart himself had to flee for his life. He quickly found a congenial refuge with Eleanor, probably about the time Henry was fighting king Stephen, and soon developed an extravagant passion for her that he made known in some of his most admired songs. A thirteenth-century biographer says that 'he was a long time at her court and he fell in love with her and she fell in love with him'. Later Bernart described himself as being 'like a man beyond hope', sighing 'in such a state of love I was, though I would come to realize that I had been a madman', that his wits fled whenever he saw the duchess, and he had 'no more sense than a child, so overcome by love was I'. He told Eleanor—whom he addressed as 'my magnet' [*mos aziman*]—'You have been the first among my joys and you shall be the last, so long as there is life in me.' In Provençal his songs have a liquid beauty that must have enchanted the duchess and her court.

According to a somewhat dubious tradition, Henry then summoned Bernart to England. A hundred years afterwards the biographer Uc de Saint-Circ explained that the duke, understandably uneasy at the poet's outpourings, took this means of removing him from his wife's court. Bernart did not enjoy England and wished he was a swallow who could fly back to Eleanor 'across the wild, deep sea'. He managed to return, but Eleanor herself was soon to go to England. In the end Bernart found a new patroness to worship—Ermengarde, viscountess of Narbonne—and finally died a monk.

There is no information about the relationship between Eleanor and Bernart other than his verses and some later and highly inaccurate chronicles, but her patronage shows impeccable literary taste. Bernart de Ventadour is generally acknowledged as one of the greatest troubadours. It is revealing that in one of his poems he compares his love for Eleanor with that of Tristan for *Izeut la blonda*, showing that the duchess and her court were already familiar with the Arthurian cycle at this early date.

Duke Henry returned from England in April 1154. He and Eleanor then went to Rouen, where for the first time she met her mother-in-law Matilda, the daughter of Henry I of England and grand-daughter of the Conqueror, and the widowed empress of Germany who had nearly become queen of England in her own right. For all her ability and her bravery, however, the arrogance of 'the lady of the English' had tipped the scales against her in a ferocious war of succession. Even so she had sometimes shown herself magnificently resourceful. Trapped in Oxford during the winter of 1142, Matilda had herself lowered down from the castle walls and then with only three knights, dressed all in white like herself, had crossed the frozen river beneath and calmly walked unseen through Stephen's camp to safety. Now she had passed all her claims to Henry, contenting herself with giving advice and helping him to govern Normandy. This splendid virago seems to have mellowed with age, and there is no record of any clash with her daughter-in-law. No doubt she recognized her as a woman of the same mettle as herself.

At last, on 25 October 1154, king Stephen died, and the news reached Rouen early in November. Terrible weather kept Henry from his kingdom for another month. Finally, despite the contrary winds, he set sail with Eleanor from Barfleur in a fever of angry impatience. The voyage must have been as miserable as those she had known on the crusade, and the ship lost contact with the fleet in a dense fog. But after twenty-four hours of storm-tossed peril she and her husband were blown on shore near Southampton.

6 Queen of England

'She made great Caesar lay his sword to bed.'

Shakespeare, *Antony and Cleopatra*

'A very clever woman, most noble of blood, but fickle.'

Gervase of Canterbury

Henry and Eleanor were crowned 'king and queen of the English' by the archbishop of Canterbury on 19 December 1154. So unanimous was the acclaim that archbishop Theobald had had no difficulty in governing the kingdom during the six weeks between Stephen's death and Henry's arrival. It was probably at the coronation that Henry received his name of 'curtmantle', on account of his waist-length French cloak, which made an odd contrast with the old-fashioned voluminous garments of the English magnates. As was customary, the new king issued a coronation charter, but it was not the usual list of concessions designed to please the great. Instead Henry II promised to restore lands and laws to what they had been at the death of his grandfather Henry I in 1135.

Presumably Eleanor was intrigued by her new country. Although she knew the Balkans, the middle east and Italy, and had experienced extremes of hot and cold weather, the damp English climate with its rain and fogs must have been an unpleasant surprise, even if summers were warmer then than they usually are today. An enthusiastic Englishman, William Fitz-Stephen, writing only twenty years later, has left an attractive picture of the London of Henry II:

> On the east stands the Tower, exceeding great and strong, whose walls and bailey rise from very deep foundations, their mortar being mixed with the blood of beasts. On the west are two strongly fortified castles, while from them there runs a great continuous wall, very high, with seven double gates, and towers at intervals along its north side. On the south, London once had similar walls and towers; but the Thames, that mighty river teeming with fish, which runs on that side and ebbs and flows with the sea, has in the passage of time washed those bulwarks away, undermining them and bringing them down. Upstream, to the west, the royal palace rises high above the river, an incomparable building ringed by an outwork and bastions two miles from the city and joined to it by a populous suburb.
> There were thirteen greater churches and 126 smaller ones.

Apparently London's outskirts were equally agreeable:

> On all sides, beyond the houses, lie the gardens of the citizens that
> live in the suburbs, planted with trees, spacious and fair, laid out
> beside each other . . . To the north are pasture lands and pleasant
> open spaces of level meadow, intersected by running waters, which
> turn mill wheels with a cheerful sound. Nearby lies a great forest
> with wooded glades full of lairs of wild beasts, red and fallow deer,
> boars and bulls.

The corn-fields produced abundant crops, and William rhap-
sodizes about the variety of food—'dishes roast, fried and boiled,
fish of every size, coarse meat for the poor and delicate for the
rich, such as venison and various kinds of birds'—to be found
every day in 'a public cook-shop' near the river. He speaks of
scholars' competitions, tournaments in boats on the river, and
many other amusements.

But one suspects that William FitzStephen was the eternally
self-satisfied Londoner, blind to any of his city's imperfections.
In reality Eleanor's London was probably dismal enough when
compared to contemporary Paris or Bordeaux, but it was her
husband's capital and she made the best of it. An abundance of
imported goods must have done much to soften its discomforts.
And many Londoners could make themselves understood in
their peculiar Anglo-Norman dialect of French. (A modern
comparison might perhaps be the difference between Austra-
lian and English.) It was a long time since Norman courtiers
had sneeringly named Henry I and his English queen 'Godric
and Godgifu' because of their partiality for Saxons. The two
peoples had intermarried so that nowadays language was a
matter of status rather than race. Every upper- and middle-
class Englishman spoke French, which was the language of
commerce as well as of the court and the castle.

King Henry had little time to ponder on the differences between the ways of life in his widespread domains. The 'nineteen

years-long winter' of his predecessor's reign had left much of England in miserable disorder. The monks of Peterborough (who had stubbornly continued to keep their chronicle in Anglo-Saxon) give an appalling picture of conditions in the fenlands, terrorized by robber barons in impregnable castles.

When the castles were built, they filled them with devils and wicked men. Then, day and night, they took people they thought had any goods—men and women—and imprisoned them, torturing them with indescribable tortures to extort gold and silver; no martyrs were ever so cruelly tortured. They were hung up by the thumbs or by the head, with weights tied to their feet. Knotted ropes were fastened round their heads and twisted till they penetrated to the brain. They put them in prisons where there were adders and toads and killed them that way too.

The monks tell of boxes in which men were crushed with stones until their ribs, legs and arms were broken, of massive chains locked around a man's neck and throat so that he could neither lie nor sit and was unable to sleep. The poor suffered no less than the rich, their oppressors killing 'many thousands' by starvation. Further, 'when the wretched folk had no more to give, they robbed and burned all the villages, so that you could easily go a whole day's journey and never find anyone occupying a village or cultivated land. Corn was dear, and meat and butter and cheese, because there was no one in the country. Many unhappy people died of starvation; some lived by begging, who had once been rich men; others fled the country.' In the west, in the north, in many midland shires, in the Thames valley and in Kent it was as bad. Indeed, when Eleanor first came to England she found a miserable land, 'where men said that Christ and his saints slept'.

Many robber barons remained undisturbed in castles they had built unlawfully—simple, easily erected affairs of earth mounds, ditches and stockades—continuing to terrorize entire districts.

In the fortnight after his coronation Henry issued a whole series of orders to deal with the problem. Illegal castles must be demolished and mercenaries must leave. Any royal lands given away by king Stephen or seized by the barons were to be restored to Henry. He is said to have pulled down over a thousand castles, and within three months nearly every mercenary had left England. William of Newburgh (the greatest of the twelfth century historians of England) says that these men were so terrified, and slipped away in so short a time, 'that they seemed to have vanished like phantoms'. All were cowed by this formidable ruler who inexorably increased his iron grip over the entire country, travelling its length and breadth, deciding law suits and punishing criminals, and reinstating men in manors of which they had been wrongfully dispossessed. In a few months he brought back the peace and order of his grandfather's day, becoming a byword for swift justice.

This was only the beginning of Henry's programme of more efficient government. He improved the existing machinery, and then created new institutions. There was a comprehensive investigation of royal dues and a methodical examination of revenue; tax collection was made more thorough and new taxes imposed, Exchequer officials receiving every encouragement. A new and purer silver coinage was issued. The administration of the common law was drastically reformed by the introduction of the assize system and the rise of local juries; judges travelled regularly through the shires, dispensing justice at set times of the year. The king also hoped to harmonize ecclesiastical and secular courts, so that the latter could deal with crimes committed by clerics. He strengthened his rule over every area of his domains, centralizing the administration at Westminster and Rouen.

Nonetheless Henry's own presence was the surest guarantee of good conduct. He was constantly in the saddle, a royal judge perpetually at assize, interviewing sheriffs and checking tax receipts. Walter Map wrote feelingly: 'Solomon says "There be

Archbishop Hubert Walter: from his tomb in Canterbury Cathedral.
Courtauld Institute.

The Plantagenet tombs at Fontevrault. *Archives Photographiques, Paris.*

three things which are too wonderful for me, yea, four which I know not: the way of an eagle in the air: the way of a serpent on a rock: the way of a ship in the midst of the sea: and the way of a man with a maid". I can add a fifth: the way of a king of England.' Peter of Blois complains how Henry was always leaving early or changing his mind so that the vast royal retinue was thrown into complete disorder—'a lively imitation of hell'. Courtiers and officials accompanying him often found when they reached their destination that there was accommodation for the king alone, and would draw their swords to fight for a hovel 'which pigs disdain'. One night, he rode over the Welsh mountains in drenching rain for sixteen hours. Peter says that sometimes the king covered in a day five times the distance a normal man thought feasible: he probably averaged as much as forty miles.

Eleanor had to accompany her husband along terrible roads that at best were the remains of those left by the Romans, at worst little tracks that became quagmires in winter or wet weather. No doubt she rode on horseback when she could, but if pregnant (which she frequently was) she must have had to endure travelling in clumsy, leather-roofed waggons with springless wooden wheels. It may have been some consolation that comforts were at hand in the wains that jolted after her: furniture, bedding, plate, table linen, hangings and curtains, even portable chapels, to make tolerable gaunt stone keeps or rough wooden halls.

In spite of all the discomfort, with such an active mind herself the queen must have admired her new partner's energy and originality, his decisiveness and stream of fresh ideas. No man could have been more different from Louis VII. Eleanor frequently dispensed justice in Henry's absence, arbitrating in disputes over land and feudal dues, and presiding over law courts. She also kept a careful watch on certain tax receipts. Throughout, she showed herself clear-headed and firm, indeed dictatorial.

In the later stages of her pregnancies and at great feasts, however, and no doubt too sometimes at her own whim, Eleanor stayed in Henry's palaces, which were probably far from uncomfortable—at least for the queen and her ladies. The most important were Westminster, Clarendon and Woodstock. Westminster was an administrative complex and the centre of royal government, with its law court and Exchequer. It had become so derelict as to be uninhabitable, but the king had it rebuilt in 1155. It was spacious enough, possessing two great halls and a range of private apartments. Clarendon was no less impressive, with a magnificent hall and an unusually capacious wine cellar. (Its overgrown and incompletely excavated site near Salisbury is one of the most inexplicably neglected of English historical monuments.) But despite such splendours as marble pillars, these sumptuous buildings were still in many ways barbarous, with rushes on the floor, and a fireplace whose smoke had to find its way out through a louvre, and lit at night by flaring torches or guttering rushlights.

Probably only the queen's bowers were proof against draughts, panelled, with tiled floors and glass windows, and furnished with silk hangings and oriental carpets. She is known to have bought cushions and tapestry when in England, and from the Pipe Rolls it seems that her apartments were lit by sweet-scented oil and perfumed with incense. She possessed gold and silver plate, brassware and table linen. According to Peter of Blois the royal household had to make do with 'half-baked bread, sour wine, stale fish and bad meat', but this can hardly have been the fate of Eleanor's ladies, as she imported quantities of her native wine from La Rochelle and her cooks made lavish use of pepper and cinnamon. Nevertheless she doubtless presided with easy aplomb over banquets in the draughty, smoky great halls.

The queen would meet all the great Englishmen of her day. These included magnates such as Robert de Beaumont, earl of Leicester, and Richard de Lucy, both former supporters of king

Stephen who had become Henry's co-justiciars (his deputies during his absences from England). Hugh Bigod always remained a secret enemy of the new king, and William of Warenne, Stephen's bastard son and earl of Surrey, claimed Norfolk from Hugh. Earl Ferrers of Derby and earl Patrick of Salisbury were also among the quarrelsome, battle-scarred veterans, who can hardly have made for a harmonious court.

Far closer to Henry—and therefore to Eleanor—were the great churchmen, not because the king was pious but because they were his chief administrators. The foremost was archbishop Theobald of Canterbury, a Benedictine monk and former abbot of Bec in Normandy of whom even St Bernard approved. Gracious and amiable, he was also learned, a product of the twelfth-century renaissance and fond of intellectuals' company; his household contained many gifted young men—four future archbishops and six future bishops—and has been compared to a small university. Indeed Theobald was one of the abler and more interesting of mediaeval archbishops of Canterbury. Never an enemy of the queen as Bernard had been, he was on the contrary a peace-maker, and must have been a source of support to her.

Theobald's chief adviser was Thomas Becket, whom he made archdeacon of Canterbury (as a deacon, not as a priest). Henry took such a liking to this brilliant and impressive man that he made him his chancellor. Thomas's successor as archbishop Theobald's right-hand man was John of Salisbury, a dedicated scholar who had studied at the French schools. His principal duty was drafting appeals to Rome, a function that soon made Henry dislike him. Another outstanding personality was Gilbert Foliot, bishop of Hereford and later bishop of London. An Anglo-Norman noble already advanced in years, he was also a Benedictine monk and had once been prior of the great abbey of Cluny in Burgundy. The king trusted him and eventually appointed him his confessor. Eleanor must have met these distinguished clerics many times, often daily.

Despite his hardworking routine, Henry II found time to share some of his wife's literary tastes. This is evident in the case of Marie of France (who may have been his half sister, the bastard daughter of Geoffrey Plantagenet), abbess of Shaftesbury in Dorset. Marie wrote *lais* (elegant narrative poems on Arthurian themes derived from Brittany) that included the tale of Tristan and Yseult. Almost certainly Marie's charming verse found favour with Eleanor, and Henry seems to have paid tribute to the queen's admiration in an unusually imaginative way. Near the palace of Woodstock, deep in the forest, he built a bower inspired by the tale of Tristan and Yseult; in the story the lovers communicated by twigs dropped by Tristan into a stream flowing through Yseult's chamber, which was in an orchard surrounded by a thick fence. At Everswell, this background was recreated, complete with spring, orchard and palisade, and in the seventeenth century John Aubrey was still able to reconstruct the plan of 'Rosamund's Bower'. For tradition wrongly made the bower and its setting—a tower and a maze, 'wondrously wrought of Daedalus's work'—the scene of Henry's later romance with Fair Rosamund. A ballad of Aubrey's time tells us that:

> Most curiously that bower was built
> Of stone and timber strong.
> A hundred and fifty doors
> Did to this bower belong.

However, it is likely that Henry had Everswell built to divert Eleanor in the early, reasonably happy, years of their marriage.

The troubadours and Marie of France were far from constituting Eleanor's entire literary patronage. Her official court reader was Wace of Jersey, who borrowed from Geoffrey of Monmouth's *History of the Kings of Britain* to compose a narrative poem in Anglo-Norman French that was largely about king Arthur—the *Roman de Brut*. For, due to Chrétien de Troyes and other poets, the legendary British monarch had become the rage of Henry's court. Some noblemen (though not king Henry) modelled themselves on Arthur's knights, and a search was made for his tomb at Glastonbury. Both the king and the queen clearly believed in the legend, and visited Glastonbury themselves; Henry told the monks where they ought to dig for Arthur's bones. Eleanor also patronized Chrétien de Troyes, whose earliest romance, *Erec et Enide*, may possibly have been inspired in part by her own adventures. Another writer of the same sort, Benoit of Sainte Maure, dedicated his *Roman de Troie* to the *riche dame de riche rei* (rich king's rich lady) and he, together with many other long-forgotten poets, must have benefited from her bounty and encouragement. Benoit speaks of 'her whose kindness knows no bounds'.

Although there is no direct evidence, one may be sure that Eleanor's recreations also included the twelfth-century equivalent of the stage. As well as plays in Latin and French, singers, dancers, mummers, acrobats, conjurers and jugglers would all have been included in such entertainment. John of Salisbury was plainly horrified by the artificiality and bawdiness of such performers, complaining that they played in all the magnates' houses in London, and he compared the situation to that which had once prevailed in Babylon. One cannot escape the inference that the royal palaces were as guilty of indecencies as those of the magnates. To judge from his objective observation of Eleanor and Louis in Italy, John was neither censorious nor puritanical, so it seems that even after her marriage to Henry the queen still retained her grandfather's frivolity and was not frightened of shocking the clergy.

Yet not all queen Eleanor's time was spent in amusement. For thirteen years she was constantly bearing children. She had five sons—William (who died aged only three), Henry, Richard, Geoffrey and John—and three daughters—Matilda, Eleanor and Joanna. Only Geoffrey and the younger daughters were born outside England. Three of the boys became kings and two of the girls queens.

Although such fertility was a sad reflection on Louis VII's manhood, it also gave credence to his suspicions that Eleanor's first marriage had been cursed by God. But there were enough ill omens for her second marriage too. The Poitevin line was thought to be unlucky, and there was the hermit's curse on all the descendants of William IX. Moreover, the Angevins themselves were hardly an auspicious stock. Henry's forebear, count Fulk Nerra (the Black), had been an unusually bloodstained warlord even by the standards of the eleventh century, and especially infamous as a plunderer of monasteries. He had bequeathed some uncomfortable legends. The worst of these was that he had married an evil spirit, Melusine, who was the daughter of Satan himself; she was said to have flown back to hell after bearing the count's children. Henry's family therefore had the distinction of being directly descended from the devil.

Despite their lineage Eleanor was no doubt optimistic about her children. The frustrated wife was turning into a possessive matriarch. Perhaps it was because she had had to wait so long for sons that she became so ferociously maternal; but her children were also a means of regaining power. They were to grow up very fond of her, even if they would sometimes fail to obey her.

7 The Angevin Empress

'Greatest of earthly princes.'
Richard FitzNigel on Henry II, *Dialogus de Scaccario*

'But in my bosom shall she never come
To make my heart her vassal.'
Shakespeare, *Antony and Cleopatra*

Although 'the Angevin empire' is a modern term, it is not far from the reality. It is true that twelfth-century Christendom recognized only two emperors—the Greek basileus at Constantinople and the German king of the Romans—and that Henry was the vassal of the king of France, who always retained a theoretical overlordship. But in terms of territory, of wealth and knights, the English king was unquestionably regarded by contemporaries as the most formidable monarch in western Europe. His wife shared his pinnacle. She had more than regained the eminence lost when Louis rejected her. With Henry she wore her crown at Lincoln at Christmas 1156, at Bury St Edmund's at Whitsun 1157 and at Worcester at Easter 1158, although the couple then solemnly placed their crowns on the cathedral altar and swore a strange oath never to wear them again.

On the other hand Eleanor possessed much less power than when she had been Louis's wife. Admittedly twelfth-century English queens were *regalis imperii participes* (sharers in the kingship); as queen regnant Eleanor was entitled to 'queen's gold', a special payment made to her on the issue of royal charters, and when Henry was out of the kingdom any writ was issued in her name and under her seal. Yet the real ruler in the King's absence was the justiciar. The most recent biographer of Henry II points out: 'There were brief periods when queen Eleanor acted as regent in her husband's absence, but she seems to have lent little more than the authority of her name to the actions of his ministers.' Moreover Henry ruled Aquitaine himself, something that Louis VII had never dared to do. Dr Warren adds: 'It may well be that her political marriage to Henry of Anjou brought her neither the power nor the influence she—a duchess in her own right—thought to be her due. She had to contend not merely with the dominating personality of her husband, but also, until 1167, with the influence of an even more proud and strong-willed woman than she herself—his mother, empress Matilda.'

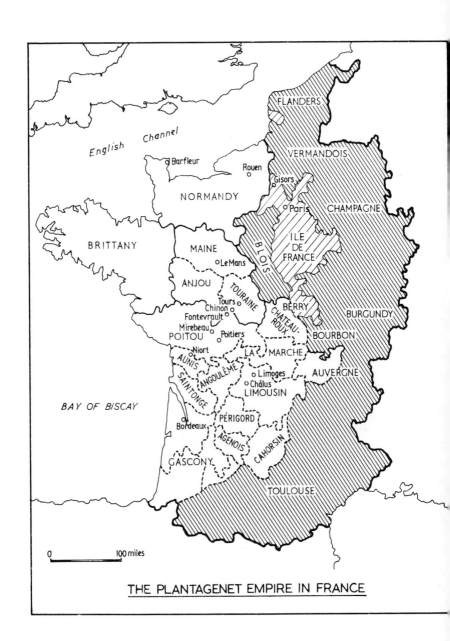

THE PLANTAGENET EMPIRE IN FRANCE

Always a realist, Eleanor soon realized that she would never be able to control this dynamic young man. No doubt, like most of his contemporaries, she found him as enigmatic as he was strong. So masterful a woman must quickly have tired of being tamed, but even if she resented it she recognized that she had met her match. She bided her time.

In any case, as has been seen, up to the late 1160s Henry kept Eleanor busy with bearing children. Eight pregnancies must have sapped even her enormous strength and vitality. Probably she solaced herself with the hope that she would recover her political power when her second surviving son, Richard, grew up and she could govern his inheritance of Aquitaine as regent. In the meantime she had to be content with mere splendour.

Eleanor's earliest rival in Henry's affections was not a woman but a man, the chancellor Thomas Becket, who had received his high office shortly after the king's accession to the throne. Born in 1118, Thomas was the son of a London merchant who had originally come from Rouen; in those days the leading London merchants ranked with barons, and the lesser ones were equated with knights. In appearance he was tall and good-looking, with a hawk-nosed pale face that reddened when he was angry or excited. As quick-witted as he was observant, he was a stimulating and amusing conversationalist. Besides studying in Paris, he had been attached to archbishop Theobald's household, whose atmosphere has been likened to a twelfth-century All Souls, but he was essentially an administrator and no intellectual. Although devout to the point of secret asceticism, he was obviously an ambitious career ecclesiastic who was thought of as a king's man in the latent struggle between the secular power and the rights of the church.

As archdeacon of Canterbury Thomas Becket had held the most important ecclesiastical position below that of bishop. Only a few weeks after obtaining it, he was made chancellor of England, probably at Christmas 1154. His contemporaries write that

Thomas stood with the king as Pharaoh did with Joseph. As his greatest biographer has observed: 'The eight years of his chancellorship are all but unique in the annals of the English monarchy between the Conquest and the age of Wolsey. At no other time did a minister of the Crown combine the assets of complete royal confidence and delegation of power with such talents of administration, of diplomacy and of display.' He even organized the demolition of the robber-barons' castles. He became a kind of grand vizier, the *alter ego* of the king who appreciated his fine mind and driving energy and relished his witty conversation. The pair spent whole days together, hunting and hawking and playing chess as well as endlessly discussing the business of the realm. Henry even entrusted to him the upbringing of his heir. For his part Thomas was plainly fascinated by the magic of royalty and the excitement of court life. Despite the fact that Henry was sixteen years the younger, a deep friendship developed between king and chancellor.

This brotherly affection can only have fuelled Eleaner's jealousy and frustration. We know that she disliked Thomas, although we have no details. As Régine Pernoud comments, 'A wife seldom warms to her husband's best friend'. Moreover the chancellor kept such a splendid and hospitable household that it was almost an alternative court to that of the queen, especially during the first year in England, when she had to stay at Bermondsey while Westminster was rebuilt and refurbished. 'He hardly ever dined without the company of sundry earls and barons. . . . His board was resplendent with gold and silver vessels and abounded in dainty dishes and precious wines', according to William FitzStephen, who clearly remembered it with nostalgia. Henry was a frequent guest, often arriving without warning. Such competition can hardly have endeared Thomas to the queen. Above all, he had taken the power that she wanted for herself—he had usurped her place as the second person in the kingdom. Indeed Thomas Becket possessed far more influence than abbot Suger had ever had. Nevertheless, Eleanor seems to have been too shrewd to show any open enmity towards him.

The queen's powerlessness is attested by the significant silence of the chroniclers. With one important exception almost nothing of importance is said about her before Henry's death, so that she has been described, with perhaps a certain exaggeration, as 'a figure of legend and romance, but not of history'; it is also true that we have no documentary evidence whatsoever about her relations with her husband until her quarrel with him in 1173. All the same, we know from the chronicles that she spent plenty of time with him and presided jointly over the court, as well as accompanying him on progress. We know too that she was with him in France; it is highly unlikely that so sensible and realistic a statesman as Henry did not ask her advice, both in dealing with king Louis and in governing Aquitaine, and her knowledge and experience must have been invaluable.

The first time that the royal couple were in France together after Henry's accession was in the autumn of 1156, when Eleanor joined him on a great progress through Aquitaine during which they held court at Bordeaux. Henceforward she was constantly crossing and re-crossing the Channel, despite the danger and discomfort of such voyages, which frequently lasted several days.

Meanwhile, her former husband had re-married. King Louis's new bride was a Spanish princess, Constance of Castile. Ironically, during her short marriage Constance bore Louis two more daughters but no sons. Both the French king and the English king now decided that a stable peace was desirable. Accordingly Thomas Becket led a splendid embassy to Paris in the summer of 1158. He was preceded by 250 foot soldiers and escorted by 200 knights and squires, with stag hounds, mastiffs and falcons, and brought a train of sumpter horses and eight vast waggons each drawn by five horses, which carried chests of gold and silver plate together with rich garments and silken hangings for presents. (There were also two carts containing what appears to have been brown ale, which, it was claimed, tasted much better than any French wine.) The awed French are said to have commented, 'The king of England must be a marvellous man if his chancellor travels with such great display'. Henry himself—without Eleanor—arrived in Paris in September. A marriage was arranged between his son and heir, Henry, and Louis's eldest daughter by his new marriage, Margaret. The dowry was the Vexin, the Norman border territory that the Plantagenet had been forced to surrender to the French king in 1152. Furthermore Louis formally gave Henry permission to reconquer the county of Nantes, which had been seized by the duke of Brittany. Later Henry took Louis on a progress through Normandy, during which the French king expressed his deep affection for him.

The marriage was a particular triumph for Eleanor. She had, after all, borne a son who might be king of France one day, unless the two daughters she had had by Louis could make good their precedence. Princess Margaret was to be brought up in England, although her father stipulated that she must never be in the custody of Eleanor.

By now Henry II had gone from success to success. He had subdued England and brought it peace, and he appeared to have pacified even the Welsh. He had acquired control of Brittany and ensured that the Vexin would eventually return to the Plantagenets. His possessions in France, including Aquitaine, were gratifyingly submissive. Understandably his ambition grew and he wanted to rule still more territory.

Like William X and William IX before him, Henry looked hopefully at the great and rich county of Toulouse. Cut off from Capetian France by the Massif Central, Toulouse had once been part of greater Aquitaine. It was especially important in that through it ran the trade routes so vital for Aquitaine's prosperity, the waterways and Roman roads that connected the

duchy with the Mediterranean. Its possession would be the ultimate rounding off of the Angevin empire, which without it
would be strategically unsound. Eleanor may well have encouraged Henry to assert the rights to Toulouse that she had inherited from her grandmother, although Henry was hardly the
man to be unaware of such a useful claim. The present count,
Raymond V, was weak and inept and at odds with his vassals,
who included the formidable count of Barcelona whose wife was
queen of Aragon; he was also on bad terms with his countess,
Constance of France, who was Louis VII's sister. In June 1159,
Henry approached the French king to obtain his agreement on a
campaign against Toulouse. Possibly to his surprise, after three
days of discussion Louis refused; but Henry ignored this setback
and at the end of the month set out with a vast army that had
been assembling at Poitiers since March. The host was large
enough for a crusade; as well as the lords of England, Normandy
and Aquitaine, it included the king of Scots (Malcolm IV), the
duke of Brittany, and even a Welsh prince, together with the
count of Barcelona and many other of Raymond's estranged vassals. So great a prize required a great army. Yet the English
king—an experienced soldier who had fought in many campaigns—disliked bloodshed and had little taste for war; nor was
he a good strategist.

Nevertheless Henry besieged and captured the fine town of
Cahors, overran the rich little county of Quercy, and in early
July laid siege to Toulouse itself. His intention seems not to have
been to capture the city or to depose Raymond, but simply to
make the count submit to his overlordship. Suddenly king Louis
intervened, showing unexpected abilities as a statesman. First,
he visited Henry to mediate; then, finding the English king obdu-
rate, he installed himself in Toulouse and took over the direction
of the defence. Henry was confounded. He had no desire to
attack his overlord, although Thomas Becket urged him to do so;
such a step meant breaking his feudal oath and, besides being

dishonourable, would provide his own vassals with a dangerous precedent. Moreover the French king, despite his lack of material resources, enjoyed a moral prestige throughout France that it was unsafe to discount. And Henry had also a curious affection for Louis; as a distinguished historian has observed, after marrying Eleanor 'Henry by turns fought, outwitted, despoiled and made friends with her sometime husband in one of the most remarkable political love-hate relationships in mediaeval Europe'. Nonetheless the English king continued to invest Toulouse even if he dared not mount an assault. At last in September he led his huge army away, having achieved nothing. He would never again be able to repeat such an expedition and had lost for ever any hope of acquiring Toulouse. He went up to Normandy, to expel invading forces led by Louis's brother, after which he negotiated a truce.

The fiasco of the Toulouse campaign marks the end of Henry's years of almost unbroken triumph. Henceforth he would have to fight constantly to keep his empire, though he was to do so with considerable success. For Eleanor of Aquitaine, however, the final loss of Toulouse must have been a still more bitter blow, the extinction of the dream of her father and grandfather. Without Toulouse, Aquitaine would always be vulnerable, an unpleasant fact that she must have clearly recognised. So masterful a woman never suffered gladly either fools or failure, and she may well have blamed Henry for not daring to attack Louis.

It was still possible, however, that her son would be king of France, a prize even greater than Toulouse. On 2 November 1160 five-year-old Henry and five-year-old Margaret were married at Rouen by papal legates. In consequence the English king obtained immediate possession of the Vexin and its fortresses, much to Louis's irritation. No doubt king Henry was uneasy. Louis's second wife had died in 1160, and with shameless haste he had taken a third bride, the sister of the count of Champagne.

For the time being, however, she remained childless.

Until the beginning of 1163, Henry continued to concentrate on affairs in France, and Eleanor was with him for most of the time. They kept Christmas together at Bayeux in 1161, a year during which the queen had given birth to another daughter, Eleanor, at Falaise. The queen was also a good deal in England, where she reigned (if not ruled) as regent. When Henry returned, it was to crush a rising in South Wales, which he did by dragging prince Rhys of Deheubarth out of his mountain lair. In July 1163 all the Welsh princes paid homage to the English king at Woodstock, acknowledging him as their overlord, as also did king Malcolm of Scotland for his lands in England. But the Welsh remained unsubdued. Henry led an expedition into Wales in 1165, but it was a disastrous failure, and only a string of strong castles on the border prevented the princes from raiding deep into England.

There were other problems besides the Welsh to plague Henry. At about this time he involved himself in his famous struggle with the Church. He was determined to assert his legal rights over it in non-spiritual matters, particularly over criminal clerics, who were escaping the full civil penalties by being tried by special ecclesiastical tribunals—the 'courts Christian'. Because of an untypical situation inherited from the Anglo-Saxon monarchy, Church and state were much more closely involved with each other in England than on the Continent, with a complex intermixing of secular and clerical admistrative machinery. The growing strength and centralization of the new Angevin monarchy on the one hand and the spiritual and intellectual renaissance of twelfth-century Catholicism on the other made conflict inevitable.

Ironically, Henry brought it to a head and intensified it by making his chancellor archbishop of Canterbury in 1162; priesting and consecration transformed Thomas Becket from a king's man into a fanatical champion of the Church's rights. In 1163

Henry was informed that over one hundred acts of manslaughter had been committed by clerics since he had come to the throne. He was outraged by Thomas's leniency in such cases. When a priest in Worcester seduced a girl and then murdered her irate father, the archbishop had him branded—a sentence hitherto unknown in the courts Christian, which went against his own claim that no cleric should be mutilated. A priest in Bedford killed a knight, and Thomas merely banished him. On the whole the archbishop probably had right on his side in the technical context, however, even if it was a very fine point. But he showed such extraordinary tactlessness and such inflexible obduracy that an argument between Church and state turned into a personal duel between archbishop and king. Henry tried to bully Thomas into submission and to make him accept a new legal code for the Church in England—the Constitutions of Clarendon, which forbade appeals to Rome. The archbishop took up the most intransigent position consistent with canon law: 'Christian princes should obey the dictates of the Church instead of preferring their own authority.' In October 1164 Thomas and the king met at Northampton, where they nearly came to blows. The archbishop fled by night and, crossing the Channel in a small open boat, took refuge in king Louis's domains. Here he remained until 1170, his partisans squabbling with Henry's prelates in endless wrangles, each side appealing to the pope.

Eleanor did not like Thomas Becket; indeed, a letter of 1165 from the bishop of Poitiers told him to expect no help from that direction. She took little part in the controversy, though on at least one occasion she seems to have tried to restrain Henry's wrath. One may guess that the intractability of both her husband and the archbishop irritated so shrewd and subtle a woman; she herself would have managed the affair very differently.

Admittedly, apart from Thomas Becket, Henry kept perfect control in England. He even managed to bring the Welsh to heel. In France too he maintained his position well enough. The tacit overlordship of Brittany, which he had extracted from king Louis, brought him especially rich dividends. In 1165, after a revolt by duke Conan IV of Brittany, Henry deposed the duke, and Conan's daughter Constance was betrothed to Henry's third surviving son, the seven-year-old Geoffrey; Henry then took possession of Brittany in Geoffrey's name, its barons paying homage to him. When war broke out again with Louis in 1167, Henry more than held his own.

Yet Plantagenet ambitions had suffered a terrible blow. On 22 August 1165, Louis VII's third wife gave him the son and heir for whom he had so long prayed, the future king Philip II Augustus. Gerald of Wales, who was a young student in Paris at the time, remembered afterwards how the birth was welcomed by the Parisians 'with joy inexpressible by human speech', how 'throughout the whole of that city there was such a din and clanging of bells and such a forest of burning candles'. An old woman told Gerald that one day the baby would bring disaster on the king of England, 'as though she was saying openly, "This night a boy is born to us who, by the blessing of God, shall assuredly be a hammer to your king"'. She spoke all too truly. Philip II was going to destroy the Angevin empire. His birth was in itself a bitter disappointment for Eleanor, the end of a dream that had lasted for nearly thirty years. Now no son of her's would ever be king of France.

8 The Court at Poitiers

'Love rules the court.'
Sir Walter Scott, *The Lay of the Last Minstrel*

'Car nulhs autres jois tant no'm plai
Cum jauzimens d'amor de lonh.'
(For no joys so please my mind
As those of loving from afar.)

Jaufre Rudel

At Oxford on Christmas Eve 1167, Eleanor gave birth to her last child, the future king John. Perhaps she did not realize that her child-bearing days were over; and if she did, she may well have been glad. Now she regained her full energies, and her magnificent constitution was unimpaired. It seems that she and Henry never again slept together. There were other reasons too why John's birth marked the end of their marriage.

Henry II was a man of strong sexual appetites. He fathered at least two bastards before his marriage: one was William 'Longsword', who became earl of Salisbury; the other was Geoffrey 'Plantagenet'—the son of a common whore called Ykenai—whom he tried to make bishop of Lincoln and who was later his chancellor and eventually archbishop of York. An item in the Pipe Rolls seems to refer to another mistress: 'For clothes and hoods and cloaks and for the trimming for two capes of samite and for the clothes of the queen and of Bellebelle.' Unfortunately nothing is known of the promisingly named Bellebelle. In the 1160s there was a nasty accusation by a rebellious Breton vassal, Eudo de Porhoet, that the king had seduced his daughter when she was his hostage. Later Henry fathered a child on a prospective daughter-in-law, and he was obviously quite ruthless in satisfying his lusts. William of Newburgh says that the king did not begin to be unfaithful to the queen until she was past child-bearing, but the statement does not carry conviction.

It is likely that Henry began his long affair with Rosamund Clifford before 1167. Unlike his other mistresses she was not merely a sleeping partner but a genuine rival to the queen. It has often been suggested that it was this affair that turned Eleanor against Henry. Yet it is just as likely that she was not altogether displeased with the affair, which left her free to intrigue. Perhaps as early as 1167 Eleanor started to hatch a vast and involved plot that would take many years of careful, secret preparation.

'Fair Rosamund' was the daughter of a knight from the Welsh border, Walter de Clifford, who had served in Henry's wars in

Wales. It has been plausibly suggested that the king may first have met her during his Welsh campaign of 1165. We know little about her except that she was young and very beautiful. According to Gerald of Wales, some contemporaries made a play on her name and called her 'Rose of the World' (*rosa-mundi*); the disdainful Gerald preferred to call her 'Rose of Unchastity'(*rosa-immundi*). The legend of her beauty persisted down the ages, as in the seventeenth-century ballad:

> Her crisped locks like threads of gold
> Appeared to each man's sight;
> Her sparkling eyes, like Orient pearls,
> Did cast a heavenly light.
>
> The blood within her crystal cheeks
> Did such a colour drive
> As though the lily and the rose
> For mastership did strive.

Legend also connects her with the palace of Woodstock. Gerald informs us that Henry was for long a 'secret adulterer' with her before he openly paraded Rosamund at his court as his mistress, presumably after his final break with Eleanor.

In the sixteenth century Michael Drayton wrote of Rosamund's labyrinth and tower at Woodstock, 'by which, if at any time her lodgings were laid about by the queen, she might easily avoid peril'. (This may have been the bower and garden at Everswell, which had originally been built for Eleanor.) The most picturesque legend of all recounts how the angry queen finally penetrated to Rosamund's refuge and offered her a choice between a dagger and a cup of poisoned wine. (Another version is that the queen arranged for her to be bled to death in a bath.) In reality Eleanor almost certainly never met her.

The greatest authority on Eleanor of Aquitaine, Edmond René Labande, makes the point that Eleanor had better things to do than to murder Fair Rosamund; instead, she revenged herself by inciting Poitou to revolt. He also emphasizes that the revolt was the culmination of a skilfully conceived plan that took a long time to reach fruition. In fact one may argue that Eleanor had little, if any, interest in revenge, and had made up her mind to rebel from the day that she realised that Henry was not going to share his power with her. She had been brought up to be a great ruler, and Henry, like Louis, had deprived her of her destiny.

There is no evidence that Henry II ever suspected his queen of harbouring the slightest disloyalty towards him. One can only conclude that the king did not understand his wife and was incapable of appreciating that women too can be greedy for power. The person who should have disillusioned him, the empress Matilda, died in 1167. Her epitaph was 'Here lies Henry's daughter, wife and mother—great by birth, greater by marriage, but greatest by motherhood'. Even her example should have been enough to put Henry on his guard, though with hindsight it is plain that Eleanor was a consummate mistress of dissimulation.

No doubt because of his affair with Rosamund, the king was anxious that Eleanor should keep out of England. He had been having trouble with her vassals in Aquitaine and he decided that her residence among them might have a calming effect. Accordingly, early in 1168 he allowed her to establish herself in Poitou, in the Maubergeon. Five happy years would pass before she had to return to England. She was back exactly where she had been when Louis divorced her—save that Henry retained ultimate authority.

As in 1153 Eleanor's journey to Poitiers was a dangerous one. The counts of Angoulême, La Marche and Lusignan and the latter's brothers—two of whom would one day wear the crown of Jerusalem—were in revolt. Henry had stormed the castle of Lusignan and, before going north on another campaign, installed Eleanor in this perilous refuge. To protect her he left in

Aquitaine Patrick, earl of Salisbury, a seasoned veteran of king Stephen's wars. One day the queen and earl Patrick were out riding when they were suddenly ambushed by the Lusignans. The earl sent Eleanor safely back to the castle, but while preparing to attack he was treacherously stabbed in the back. His nephew William, an obscure young knight, thereupon charged the Lusignan party single-handed 'like a famished lion' and was badly wounded and taken prisoner. His captors refused to dress his wounds, and he remained seriously ill. The queen heard of his plight and ransomed him, rewarding him with money, armour, horses and rich clothes—a great stroke of luck for a poor young man. But Eleanor was always discerning in her patronage. William was to become Marshal of England, the greatest soldier of his day, and to save the throne for her grandson.

Eleanor finally re-installed herself in the Maubergeon, to begin one of the most agreeable periods of her life. At last she had regained some sort of freedom. During this time an enormous and very beautiful hall was added to the ducal palace. It still stands—now the Palais de Justice of Poitiers—as do several other buildings that she must have known well, such as the Romanesque church of Notre Dame la Grande with its exquisite facade. Poitiers itself, on its cliff and defended by massive ramparts, was a safe and splendid city. The queen's court there was full of poets, including such troubadours as Gaucelm Faidit, Rigaut de Barbezieux, Bertran de Born and her old admirer Bernart de Ventadour, and men from the north such as Chrétien de Troyes. It has been suggested that Marie of France also came over from England to Poitiers. There were tournaments, plays and feasting, and those romantic song contests over which Eleanor herself presided, which were later described as courts of love.

Sometimes the queen's place at these contests was taken by her eldest child, Marie of Champagne, who shared her mother's tastes to a marked degree. Marie was an enthusiastic follower of the Arthurian cult and a considerable literary patroness in her own right; the troubadour Rigaut calls her 'the gay and joyous countess' and 'the light of Champagne'. She encouraged Chrétien de Troyes to write his *Lancelot*, in which the great knight overcomes every danger to win queen Guinevere's heart and submits to every humiliation with which she tests him.

The principal entertainment at the court of Poitiers was of course the *gai saber* (joyous art) of the troubadours. It is important to understand what this meant in terms of human relationships. The troubadour's exaggerated devotion to a high-born lady beyond his reach—his 'service of love'—had a certain analogy to the vassal's loyalty to his overlord. There were four stages in the troubadour's ritual courtship: first, that of the *fegnedor* (aspirant); second, that of the *precador* (suppliant); third, that of the *entendedor* (acknowledged suitor); and fourth, that of the *drut* (recognized lover). When he achieved the last stage, the troubadour sealed his fidelity by an oath and the lady her acceptance by a kiss. He then wrote songs about his beloved, whose identity was kept secret by a pseudonym, singing that she was so perfect that her beauty lit up the night, healed the sick, made the sad happy, and turned louts into courtiers. He complained how separation from her meant death and how his love for her had totally transformed him, and he threatened that if she would not love him in return he could not eat or sleep, but would soon die from misery. In theory the relationship was purely platonic.

The 'courts of love' were the troubadour's real audience, apart from his lady herself. They were essentially a court game whose most obvious expression was the *tenso*, a two-part song. In this, one troubadour would sing a stanza about a problem that his love had encountered, whereupon another troubadour would sing a second stanza giving his opinion, after which the performance would be repeated. Usually, neither could decide and they would then agree to submit to the judgment of some great lady.

Nineteenth-century literary historians were misled by the

phrase 'courts of love', and mistakenly imagined them as some sort of feudal tribunal. Their error is understandable, however, since so little evidence survives. One of the only sources is the far from reliable André le Chapelain, who wrote in the thirteenth century, when the age of troubadours and courts of love was long over. Another, even further removed, is the sixteenth-century writer Nostradamus (brother of the famous astrologer), who pretended to derive his information from a manuscript composed by a fictitious 'monk from the isles of gold'. But Nostradamus had access to many genuine Provençal manuscripts that have since perished. Moreover, if distorted, much of what André le Chapelain has to say in his strange treatise on love is obviously fairly near the truth. He claims to describe the formal code for the troubadours' love affairs, professedly derived from that of king Arthur's knights. Based on Ovid and even more openly erotic, it stands the Roman poet on his head: instead of the knight being the seducer, he is the lady's slave; and far from a woman being male property, a man becomes female property. André mentions some of the judgments given in the courts of love—against a lady who had set her lover too stern a task, and that it is doubtful whether love in its truest sense can exist between husband and wife. Beyond question his treatise does preserve something of the curious and esoteric atmosphere of the court of Eleanor and her daughter.

Eleanor herself was still the lady of many troubadours. Helen Waddell quotes what 'is surely the work of a German student, haunted by a passing glimpse of Eleanor of Aquitaine, and perhaps as surely her slave as Bertran de Born'. He sings:

> Were the world all mine
> From the sea to the Rhine,
> I'd give it all
> If so be the queen of England
> Lay in my arms.

However genuine, this naïve *minnesinger* can scarcely have been
so impressive a conquest as Bertran de Born, who was still in his
twenties in the 1160s. When not a gentle, sighing troubadour
strumming on his lute, Bertran was a bloodthirsty robber-baron
who drove his own brother out of the family castle of Altafort in
the Dordogne. He was only happy when making verses or war.
Later he became the bosom friend of the queen's eldest son
Henry, and was credited by some with leading him into rebellion.
Indeed Dante placed him in hell for doing so:

> Sappi ch'io son Bertram dal Bornio quelli
> Che diedi al re giovane mai conforti.
> Io feci il padre e il figlio in sè ribelli.

> (Bertram dal Bornio, be it known, am I
> Who urged the young king to rebel.
> Father and son at enmity I set.)

It may have been a fond memory of his adoration for Eleanor
that caused Bertran to revolt.

The courtiers of queen Eleanor's unreal world at Poitiers
dressed fantastically, as was fitting. 'They have clothes of rich
and rare materials, in colours chosen to match their moods', the
contemporary chronicler Geoffrey of Vigé tells us, 'they flaunt
slashed cloaks and flowing sleeves like hermits. Young men grow
their hair long and wear shoes with pointed toes'. Geoffrey also
adds that one might mistake the ladies for snakes, because of the
enormously long trains that they drag after them. Moreover a
precursor of the Rue de la Paix clearly existed in Eleanor's Poitiers. Among suitable presents to give to a lady, André le Chapelain lists fine handkerchiefs, circlets of gold or silver, brooches,
small looking glasses, purses, girdles, combs, sleeves, gloves,
rings, caskets, and almost anything else that might be of use for
her toilet or on her dressing table.

Marie of Champagne was not the only great lady to support

Eleanor at the court of Poitiers. There was also the queen's other daughter by Louis VII, Alice of Blois, together with her niece (the countess of Flanders) and Ermengarde, viscountess of Narbonne. It was indeed a most regal court, and suitably it was visited by kings. In June 1172 Eleanor received both Alfonso II of Aragon and Sancho VI of Navarre—though for this she took her courtiers to Limoges.

From time to time the queen saw her husband. She kept Christmas with Henry at Bures near Bayeux in 1170 and at Chinon in Touraine in 1172. He still insisted on retaining ultimate control of Aquitaine. He is known to have visited the duchy in 1170 and again early in 1173, governing personally and dispensing justice as though he were the duke. One can only guess at Eleanor's fury: not even in her own land did she enjoy real power. But the king does not seem to have noticed any resentment on her part, or else he simply ignored it. It is more than probable that his wife concealed her anger. For, secretly, she was suborning the lords of Aquitaine and Poitou, making sure that their first loyalty was to their duchess and not to the king of England.

9 Eleanor's Sons

'From the Devil they came and to the Devil they will go.'

St Bernard

'She is cunning past man's thought.'

Shakespeare, *Antony and Cleopatra*

In January 1169, Henry II and Louis VII met at Montmirail in Maine to negotiate (it was hoped) a lasting peace settlement. For two years both kings had been engaged in a futile war that, while being both expensive and destructive, had gained no advantage for either. Among other matters an attempt was made to reconcile Henry with Thomas Becket, but both king and archbishop were incapable of compromise. The principal business, however, was to secure Louis's agreement to Henry's plans for a dynastic settlement that would divide the Angevin empire among his sons and enable him to ensure the local barons' recognition of their right to succeed. The settlement would also help the English king to subdue rebellious vassals who, in almost every part of his French domains, had recently been so troublesome. Louis agreed readily, only too pleased to guarantee the future division of his overmighty neighbour's empire. Eleanor, of course, was not consulted. But she must have seen in Montmirail her opportunity to overthrow her husband and to regain complete independence.

The eldest surviving Plantagenet son, Henry, was to have England, Normandy, Maine and Anjou—his father's own inheritance—together with the overlordship of Brittany. To ensure his undisputed succession, the Capetian custom was adopted of crowning the fifteen-year-old boy king in his father's lifetime. The coronation took place on 24 May 1170 in Westminster Abbey and was performed by the archbishop of York (Thomas Becket having refused an invitation to return to England to do so). No pomp was lacking, the crown made by the London goldsmith William Cade costing £38 6s 0d—an enormous sum for the period. His wife Margaret—Louis's daughter—was not crowned with him, a strange and insulting omission. At the coronation banquet the old king, as he was henceforth to be known, waited on the young king. The archbishop of York commented unctuously that no prince in all the world was waited on by a king. The youth replied, 'It is not unfitting that the son of a mere count should wait on the son of a king'. The retort tells us a good deal about the young king, who was both conceited and ungrateful. From now on he had his own household, and contemporary writers refer to him as 'Henry III', an eloquent testimony as to how seriously they took his kingship. It is said that Eleanor was delighted by her son's elevation. There was, it is clear, considerable affection between her and the young king, who sometimes visited Poitiers with his wife. No doubt the queen was already working to make him her ally against the old king.

We know nothing about Eleanor's relations with her children during their childhood. According to the custom of the age they would have been brought up away from her, first by foster-mothers and then in the households of trusted magnates, although she must have seen them all from time to time. Nevertheless it is possible that she saw more of Richard, the fourth child of her second marriage, and from a very early age, because—as the heir to Aquitaine from his cradle—he was the very centre of her hopes of regaining power. From the time of Montmirail at least, when he was still only twelve, he was Eleanor's constant companion. In view of his later reputation for homosexuality, it is not too much to suppose that the queen was one of those excessively dominant mothers who transform their sons into little lovers; after leaving Henry she did not indulge in love affairs nor did she have any notably close male friends, and it is likely that Richard was the only man in her life and she the only woman in his.

At Montmirail Louis both recognized Richard's claim to Aquitaine and betrothed him to Alice, his daughter by his second marriage, who was sent to England to be brought up. No doubt Eleanor rejoiced when, in that same year of 1169, king Henry ordered that Richard be proclaimed count of Poitiers; and in the summer of the following year he was consecrated as count, and recognized as future duke of Aquitaine, in a series of splendid ceremonies. At Niort he was presented to the nobles of the region, who paid homage to him. At Poitiers in the cathedral of Saint-Hilaire, before his greatest vassals, he received from the city's bishop and the archbishop of Bordeaux the holy lance and banner of Saint-Hilaire; he was also created abbot of Saint-Hilaire. There was a third ceremony at Limoges in the abbey of Saint-Martial, where the bishop of Limoges placed on his betrothal finger the ring of St Valerie, the Roman martyr who was the city's patron saint. All these ceremonies were accompnied by oaths sworn on the gospels and by pontifical high Masses, followed by banquets and jousting. (Gervase of Canterbury and Geoffrey of Vigé are incorrect in saying that Richard was instituted as duke of Aquitaine as well as count of Poitiers; he did not receive Aquitaine until 1179.) Eleanor had good reason to rejoice. Despite his homosexuality Richard was to prove the strongest and most worthwhile of her sons.

Geoffrey, the third surviving son, had been recognized by king Louis at Montmirail as heir to Brittany, which he would hold as a vassal of the king of England. As has been seen, he had acquired his claim to the duchy by his betrothal to the daughter of the deposed duke Conan. His position was strengthened by Conan's death in 1170, when Henry annexed the former duke's county of Penthièvre in Geoffrey's name, and by the confiscation during the same year of the estates of the great Breton rebel Eudo de Porhoet. Geoffrey grew up to be one of the most evil of the Plantagenets, and once boasted that it was the tradition of his family for brother to hate brother and for a son to turn against his father. He too was to have no qualms about rebelling against Henry, which was all to Eleanor's purpose. Like the young king, Geoffrey visited his mother's court at Poitiers.

The fourth son, John, received nothing at Montmirail. The king laughingly named him 'Lackland' but obviously meant to give him some great appanage in due course—much to the disquiet of his brothers, who feared that they would have to contribute towards it from their own territories.

As for Eleanor's daughters by Henry, Matilda married duke Henry of Saxony, one of the greatest of the German princes, in 1168; Eleanor was betrothed to Alfonso VIII of Castile in 1170; and Joanna, the youngest, married William II of Sicily in 1177. None of these girls played any part in their mother's grand design.

Meanwhile the affair of Thomas Becket finally blew up in Henry II's face in 1170. Although the dispute had not been settled, and despite warnings, the archbishop insisted on returning to England where he was as noisily intransigent as ever. At his Christmas court at Bures in Normandy, where Eleanor was keeping him company, Henry cursed his maddening archbishop; perhaps he did not actually say, 'Will no one rid me of this turbulent priest?', but clearly he said something very like it. Four of his magnates—not mere knights—set out to do so, despite vain efforts to stop them by messengers whom the king sent in pursuit. On the night of Tuesday 29 December they hacked the archbishop to death in his own cathedral at Canterbury, deliberately spilling the brains out óf his skull onto the pavement. The killing horrified all Christendom. Pope Alexander III would not allow Henry's name to be mentioned in his presence for a week after hearing the news, Louis VII called him a 'rebel against humanity', and the count of Blois spoke of a 'horrible . . . unparalleled crime'. Although Henry was not excommunicated and his kingdom was not laid under an interdict, he had to undergo many humiliations that culminated in 1174 with his being scourged at the archbishop's tomb by the monks of Canterbury. Naturally his enemies, including Eleanor, believed that his power had been severely undermined.

Moreover at this most inauspicious time the English king appeared to be over-extending his resources by attempting to conquer Ireland, the most barbarous land in Christendom. It was ruled by countless petty kinglets or chieftains, who paid a loose allegiance to five over-kings and an elected 'high king', in a society very like that which existed in the Scottish Highlands before 1746. Their principal occupation was fighting and cattle raiding, but they were usually incapable of uniting against a common foe. The only towns were a few seaports founded by the Vikings and peopled by their descendants, and the island's sole wealth was its rich pastureland; much of the country was covered by impenetrable bog and forest. The only exports were wolfhounds and pine marten skins. For a brief period during the Dark Ages the Irish Church had been famed for its saints and scholars, but that was now a thing of long ago save for a few newly established Cistercian monasteries. Irish morals scandalized Christendom; bishops were frequently succeeded by their sons, and the native Brehon law recognized six sorts of marriage, most of them concubinage. The pope had almost no authority in this anarchic and savage land. Henry had contemplated invading it as early as 1155 and had obtained a grant of 'lordship' over Ireland from the English pope Adrian IV, whose own motive was to impose proper clerical discipline. For all its poverty and barbarity, its rains and mists, here plainly was another country for Normans to conquer, just as they had done in England and Sicily. From 1169 Norman marcher lords from Wales were operating in Ireland; in 1170 they captured Dublin, its richest town, and during the next year overran its eastern coast as far south as Waterford. King Henry had no desire to see the establishment of a new and independent Norman-Irish state that would not be subject to him. In October 1171, therefore, he landed near Waterford, remaining in Ireland until the following April and extorting homage from the Norman invaders and from many of the native kings. Although he never visited it again, he was henceforth to devote much time, effort and wealth to the conquest and settlement of Ireland.

Henry's domains now stretched across a second sea. His vassals were some of the most unruly and turbulent in Europe—

fiery Occitanians, Poitevins and Angevins, dour Normans and English, and wild Bretons, Welsh and Irish. Hardly a day went by without rebellion in some corner of his ramshackle empire. Eleanor cannot be blamed for supposing that her husband had over-reached himself, and that a concerted revolt in as many areas as possible would bring the whole rickety structure of his power base crashing down. For such a revolt she required allies who had a genuine sense of grievance and who would band together in a carefully planned campaign. By 1173 the queen had them—her three eldest sons. She must have waited impatiently for them to grow old enough to join her.

Henry, the young king, was now eighteen. He was tall and handsome, charming and generous, and useless—'a restless youth, born for the undoing of many'. He was unquestionably brave and energetic, and a superbly chivalrous knight; William Marshal, no mean authority, calls him 'the beauty and flower of all Christian princes'. But he was hopelessly unstable, as inconstant 'as wax'. Moreover, although the young king was famed for his generosity, he was ruinously extravagant, endlessly demanding money from his father, and always in debt and borrowing recklessly. Indeed Geoffrey of Vigé says bluntly that he was 'not so much generous as prodigal', and Robert of Torigny simply terms him 'a spendthrift'. Admittedly his extravagance had a certain regal panache. Once he invited every knight in Normandy named William to dinner, and more than a hundred came. His unrestrained warmth of manner, caressing speech and wild liberality, together with his love of splendour, jousting and feasting, attracted a wide following of immature young men, the only one of any distinction being the heroic William Marshal. His protégés included that inveterate trouble-maker, Bertran de Born. Even the young king's good qualities were spoilt by excess; he was so merciful that Gerald of Wales labels him 'the shield of the wrongdoer'. The old king treated the young king with outward respect and was fond of him; in 1172 he accorded him the honour of a crown-wearing at Winchester, when his wife was consecrated queen. But although the young king was joint monarch with his father, he had no lands of his own and had to live on what he considered a shamefully inadequate allowance. The old king refused his request to let him have either England, Normandy or Anjou, and in his father's absence England was ruled by a justiciar. Even the members of his household were chosen for him. The vain young king deeply resented what he regarded as his humiliating situation.

Richard, count of Poitou, was an advanced sixteen, tall, handsome and reddish-haired like his elder brother, but stockier and stronger in build, a better horseman and (later) an infinitely better soldier. In character he was already quite different: bold, daring, harsh, with a violent and sometimes cruel streak, prone to fits of terrible Angevin rage, touchy and unforgiving. Gerald of Wales likens him to a hammer. Although good-looking, he had his father's ferocious, bulging grey eyes. Unlike the young king he was bored by tournaments, although he had a natural and savage taste for real warfare in which, even at this early age, he showed no mercy to his adversaries. On the other hand, he had his mother's love of music and poetry, wrote excellent songs in both the Poitevin dialect of French and Provençal and composed tunes for them, sang in choirs and enjoyed the company of troubadours. Later Bertran de Born was to become a close friend and gave him the Provençal nickname of *Oc-e-no* (yea-and-nay), though he could be single-minded enough. He had a respect and affection for his mother that was probably excessive, and no doubt deep sympathy for her wrongs, imagined or otherwise; but he had little love for his father. Indeed from his youth Richard was the most formidable of Eleanor's sons; he, too, wanted more power and more independence.

Her third son, Geoffrey, was only fifteen, though he too was precocious. Dark haired and not as tall as Henry or Richard, he was perhaps the most intelligent of the family and certainly the most untrustworthy. Benedict of Peterborough referred to him, when he had grown into a charming and thoroughly evil man, as 'a son of iniquity and perdition', and even as a boy Geoffrey must have been dangerous enough. He wanted to enjoy his wife's duchy of Brittany at the earliest possible opportunity.

By 1173, therefore, Eleanor's plan was ready. She had decided that, young as they were, her three rather alarming elder sons were capable of leading her revolt. Henry's wife and children prepared to overthrow him.

10 *Eleanor's Revolt*

'Note here how God stirreth up the wife of his
own bosom, and the sons descending of his own
loins, to be thorns in his eyes and goads in his
sides.'

Holinshed on Henry II in 1173

'What peace, so long as the whoredoms of thy
mother Jezebel and her witchcrafts are so many?'
The Second Book of Kings

The great revolt of 1173 against Henry II is often seen as a spontaneous rising by the angry young king, joined on the spur of the moment by all the old king's enemies within and without his domains. But it was so general and so concerted that one has to conclude that it was carefully planned in advance. The young king was too scatterbrained to do this, and his brothers, though precocious, were still too juvenile. Even if there is no firm documentary evidence, all the circumstances point to Eleanor as the architect of an ingenious plot. Its basic object was to obtain appanages for the young princes, with no strings attached, and so to weaken Henry that he would never be able to reassert his authority. Indeed, the plotters intended if possible to depose him. The queen's prize was to be Aquitaine, which she would rule through and with her beloved Richard. Only a blunder by the inane young king saved Henry.

It is clear that, until the revolt broke out, the king of England had not the slightest suspicion that his wife was plotting against him. From Roman times until the sixteenth century and the age of Elizabeth and Catherine de Medici, almost no European woman played a leading part in politics. They intrigued and occasionally succeeded in turning their menfolk against someone they disliked, but that was all. The outstanding exceptions were the empress Matilda and Eleanor of Aquitaine. The first failed because of her arrogance and lack of subtlety. Eleanor failed too, but not from any shortcomings of her own; she had bad luck and she faced an exceptionally skilful and vigorous opponent. One can only suppose that so uncannily shrewd a man as Henry II underestimated her simply because she was a woman. Yet, with a mother like Matilda, he ought to have known better.

Clearly, Eleanor dissembled over a long period of years during which she was planning to attack her husband. Perhaps one should not blame her too much. For two decades he had deprived her of her independence and power. She was like some Victorian heiress who had fallen into the clutches of a fortune-hunter

127

before the Married Woman's Property Act; although this is an anachronistic simile, it nonetheless conveys something of the resentment that she felt. She was not unnatural: Henry had forfeited any claim to her loyalty by his repeated adulteries and, above all, by taking a mistress who was a lady and a rival. Moreover he himself was always ready to break his word, so Gerald of Wales tells us, and Thomas Becket once described him as a Proteus in slipperiness.

By 1173, men throughout Henry's territories, in both England and France, had grown heartily sick of his oppressively efficient rule. In England—according to the dean of St Paul's, Ralph of Diceto—men were joining the young king's party because his father 'was trampling on the necks of the proud and haughty' and demolishing robber-barons' castles, and because 'he condemned traitors to exile, punished robbers with death, terrified thieves with the gallows, and mulcted the oppressors of the poor with the loss of their own money'. The dean's was an exceptionally loyal and charitable view. It is likely that all too many of Henry's barons thought that he was heavy handed, especially in Aquitaine, where he must have been disliked as a northerner and as a tyrant; he was savagely autocratic compared with William IX, and tolerated only because he was Eleanor's husband. Meanwhile the rebels whom he had put down in Maine and in Brittany a few years previously were biding their time.

The conspirators had a valuable ally in Eleanor's former husband. Louis VII had matured considerably, both as a statesman and as a politician. Although a lesser man than Henry II, and certainly not so gifted, he was slowly and quietly improving his position in France; he was even strengthening the power of the crown against the Church, despite his piety, and controlling episcopal elections as well as asserting royal rights, though without any of the Plantagenet's noisy disputes. Indeed Louis had lost much of his naivety, even something of his innocence. The constant menace from Henry and his vast empire, together with threats by unruly vassels inside his own borders, had developed considerable powers of survival in the French king, who was determined that the Capetian monarchy should overcome all obstacles. In particular he had acquired the most unsaintly habit of escaping from dangerous situations by proclaiming truces and then breaking them. The settlement at Montmirail had given him the tantalizing if distant prospect of a division of the Angevin empire. Eleanor's design of a grand rebellion promised to hasten the process. Although no record has survived, it is logical to conclude that secret ambassadors had been passing between Louis on the one hand and Eleanor and her sons on the other. When the young king of England visited him in the autumn of 1172, Louis told the boy to insist on being given one of his father's territories.

Henry suspected nothing. The betrothal of his daughter to the king of Castile in 1170 had effectively put an end to any danger of a Franco-Castilian alliance, besides strengthening his position vis-à-vis Toulouse. As we have seen, in 1171–2 he had been gratifyingly successful in establishing a bridgehead in Ireland. Also in 1172 he had made his peace with the Church at Avranches, where he had sworn that he had neither desired nor ordered the murder of Thomas Becket and reached an agreement with the churchmen that was more compromise than surrender. In 1172 too he had made a placatory gesture towards Louis by having the French king's daughter crowned with the young king. He had every reason to believe that he was safe from attack.

In February 1173 at Montferrand, Henry and the young king met count Humbert of Maurienne to negotiate a marriage between Humbert's heiress and John Lackland. The count ruled Savoy and Piedmont, controlling several Alpine passes from France into Italy. This was of vital concern to Henry, because the papacy (at odds with Frederick Barbarossa) was seriously considering offering him the imperial crown. That Henry was interested in so ambitious an adventure shows how he felt about the security of his own territories. He therefore promised count Humbert that John would receive the three castles on the Loire that were the customary appanage of a younger son of the house of Anjou—Chinon, Loudun and Mirabeau. This infuriated the young king, who angrily told his father that he had no right to make such a gift without his joint-sovereign's approval and that he would never agree to it. The old king, hardly the man to be browbeaten, refused to change his mind. Furthermore he at once ordered certain young knights, whom he considered a bad influence, to leave his son's household.

The young king had also demanded either England, Normandy or Anjou, as Louis had suggested. Perhaps now, for the first time, Henry began to suspect that some sort of plot was in the wind. Already he seems to have received a warning from Raymond of Toulouse that his family were plotting to depose him, but apparently he disregarded so notoriously treacherous and unreliable an opponent. Nevertheless, from the young king's outburst he may well have suspected that Louis VII was trying to make trouble between father and son. Henry thought of imprisoning the young king, but decided against it. Then, on the night of 7 March 1173, at Chinon, the young king made his guards drunk and fled north, riding for the coast as though he intended to cross the Channel and raise England. When he reached Normandy however, he changed his mind and went to Paris instead to take refuge with Louis. By his stupid outburst and subsequent flight the young king had alerted his father and, ultimately, doomed his mother's plot to failure. But the old king did not yet appreciate the full extent of the conspiracy.

Henry II sent to Paris, demanding the return of his son. Louis's reply was both a curious piece of humour and a declaration of war. When the English ambassadors said they had come from the king of England, Louis answered: 'Impossible. The king of England is with me. You are quite wrong in giving the title to his father. That king is dead and it would be as well if he ceased to think of himself as a king since before all the world he has handed over his kingdom to his son.' A council of the barons of France was summoned to Paris; they swore solemnly to fight for the young king, who in turn pledged himself to make no peace without their approval. He promised the earldom of Kent to the count of Flanders and wide lands in Touraine to the count of Blois. The council declared unanimously that 'he who was once king of England is king no longer'. A seal was specially cut for the young king on Louis's orders, so that he could convert his verbal promises into formal grants. By now Richard and Geoffrey were also in Paris, with their mother's encouragement.

The young king found allies throughout the Angevin empire. In England, the earls of Norfolk, Leicester, Chester, Derby and Salisbury, together with the lesser lords, hired mercenaries, put their castles into a state of defence, and began to attack the old king's supporters. In addition, king William the Lion of Scotland and his brother began to raid over the border. If Henry had received a single serious defeat there would probably have been a general rising throughout England. So worried was the old king that at one moment he offered the young king half England, and Richard half Aquitaine. In Poitou and Aquitaine his seneschals and castellans were expelled, and the barons, led by the count of Angoulême and the Lusignans, rose against the consort whom their duchess had repudiated. There were risings too in Normandy, Brittany, Maine and Anjou. The declared aim of Louis, and no doubt of Eleanor as well, was to strip Henry of every one of his domains save Normandy. Few rulers have suddenly found themselves so isolated, or been faced by so co-ordinated an opposition.

Henry survived. Without the young king's loss of nerve, which had set off the conspiracy prematurely, Henry might well have been seized and deposed before he had a chance to resist. As it was, most of the actual fighting took place in Normandy (which had remained largely loyal to him), in northern England and in

Brittany. Henry first threw a French invading force out of Normandy and then turned to smash the Breton rebels before crossing to England. Here his supporters, together with peasants armed with scythes and clubs, scattered the earl of Leicester's mercenaries at Fornham in Suffolk in October 1173, and by the end of the year English rebels held out only in the north and in the midlands. In the spring of 1174 a scouting party captured the king of Scots in a Northumberland fog, and by the summer the party of the young king of England had been completely broken. Meanwhile Louis and the Plantagenet princes were besieging Rouen. With an army that included Welsh mercenaries, Henry re-crossed the Channel, raised the siege, and drove the enemy out of his territories. By the autumn of 1174 it was clear that he had defeated the grand alliance: on 8 September a peace conference began at Gisors.

The old king, who knew when to compromise, was generous: the young king was given two Norman castles and an annual allowance of £1500; Richard recieved two castles in Poitou together with half the county's revenues; and Geoffrey—who, like Richard, was forgiven on account of 'his tender age'—obtained half the revenues of Brittany. But the old king insisted on his right to provide for John, giving him lands on both sides of the Channel. In appearance, at any rate, his sons had been taught a stern lesson: 'Thus the mighty learned that it was no easy task to wrest Hercules's club from his hand', exulted their father's treasurer.

The settlement made no mention of the arch-conspirator. Eleanor had been in Henry's hands for over a year. When in August 1173 her husband had first begun to retaliate in Poitou, she had taken refuge in the castle of Faye-la-Vineuse, the stronghold of her devoted uncle, Raoul of Faye. Already the archbishop of Rouen, Rotrou of Warwick, had sent her a stern letter, ordering her to return to Henry, and to cease setting his sons against him, 'otherwise you will be the cause of general ruin'. Faye-la-Vineuse soon fell to Henry's soldiers, but Eleanor fled in time. Quite by chance, on the road to Chartres and almost within sight of the Ile-de-France, some of Henry's troops intercepted a group of knights riding towards Paris. Among them, riding astride and dressed as a nobleman, was the fifty-year-old queen. She spent the next few months immured in a tower of her husband's castle of Chinon in Touraine.

11 The Lost Years

'Foolish woman, thou art now like a
firebrand that hath kindled others
and burnt thyself.'

Ford, *'Tis Pity She's a Whore*

'O sovereign mistress of true melancholy.'

Shakespeare, *Antony and Cleopatra*

Henry II's fury with his queen must have known no bounds. She was revealed at last as a secret enemy of many years, who had plotted to depose him and unleashed against him the greatest danger of his life. Admittedly he had been unfaithful to her, but—as no doubt he saw it—that was hardly sufficient reason for her to bear such enmity towards the father of her children. Reconciliation was impossible after treachery such as this. That her plot had so very nearly succeeded demonstrates how formidable she was as a politician. It is also a testimony to her lust for power.

In July 1174 Eleanor was shipped from Barfleur (possibly in the *Esnecca*—or 'snake'—which was the king's personal vessel). According to the chronicler the weather was stormy, but she survived the crossing and was confined first in Winchester and then in Old Sarum castle. Here the tower's site can still be made out within the ring of the grassy mound which is all that remains of the castle.

Henry's problem was what to do with this treacherous wife. At first he seems to have been determined to divorce her, according to Roger of Howden. On 31 October 1175 a papal legate, cardinal Uguccione Pierlone of Sant' Angelo, met the king at Winchester to discuss Church-state relations and tidy up the last vestiges of the Becket affair. It was rumoured that they were also discussing the possibility of a divorce. This posed many problems, however: to leave Eleanor free again would be to commit exactly the same political blunder that Louis VII had made nearly a quarter of a century before. Gerald of Wales believed that Henry offered the queen a divorce, but on condition that she should abandon the world and take vows as a nun; she would then be installed as abbess of the monastery of Fontevrault, of which she was so fond. Furthermore Gervase of Canterbury heard that the cardinal had been given large sums of money by the king, presumably to put him into an accommodating frame of mind, because he was noted for his avarice. The stumbling block was Eleanor herself. Despite her affection for Fontevrault, she was not going to solve her husband's difficulties by abandoning her rights, and she refused. Although she was fifty-three—which was almost old age in the twelfth century—and although all her plans lay in ruins, she would not give way to despair and accept that she no longer had any chance of regaining the slightest vestige of power. In the event her determination was rewarded; but first she had to endure fifteen years of imprisonment, or at best semi-confinement, usually in strongly fortified buildings from which there was no hope of escape.

These years were not all spent at the same place, though Winchester seems to have been the most usual. Sometimes she was moved to Ludgershall or back to Old Sarum or to other castles in Berkshire, Buckinghamshire and Nottinghamshire. Her gaolers were her husband's most trusted men, notably the great justiciar Ranulf de Glanvill, and William FitzStephen, who was one of the royal judges (and the biographer of Thomas Becket). The chronicles are almost silent about her during her imprisonment, and the few entries in the Pipe Rolls suggest that little was spent on her upkeep, in miserable contrast to the luxury that she had known all her life. But even if she pined for Poitou, nothing could break her extraordinary spirit.

Henry was now openly living with Rosamund Clifford, but she did not enjoy her triumph for long. In 1176 she fell ill and took up residence in the nunnery of Godstow, where she soon died; she had become a nun, perhaps on her deathbed. In all save beauty Fair Rosamund had been the opposite of Eleanor, showing no taste whatsoever for politics or power. She was interred before the convent altar and her tomb became a sort of shrine, decked with silken cloths and carefully tended by the nuns according to the provision of Henry's endowment. In 1191, two years after Henry's own death, that stern Carthusian bishop St Hugh of Lincoln visited Godstow and was horrified to find that the community still venerated the grave; he had her corpse removed to the cemetery—'because she was a harlot', Roger of Howden explains. Henry II's latest biographer says of Rosamund, 'undoubtedly she was the great love of his life'. He may even have thought of making her his queen instead of Eleanor. He continued to take mistresses, but none of them filled Rosamund's place in his affections.

Eleanor must have known very little about what was happening in the world outside her prisons—a wretched deprivation for so active a mind. Perhaps her gaolers were kind enough to let her know of the betrothal of her daughter Joanna (born in 1165) to king William II of Sicily in July 1176; Joanna travelled overland to her new kingdom, where she married William in February the following year; her lot as a wife cannot have been altogether agreeable, as her husband kept a harem like those of his Saracen subjects. As for Eleanor's sons after they had made peace with their father, Richard waged a long and bloody campaign against the rebels who had formerly supported him, and to such effect that in the autumn of 1176 he stormed Angoulême and sent its count to England to implore Henry's pardon on his knees. In 1178 her husband met Louis VII at Ivry and swore, though no doubt with scant sincerity, to go on a joint crusade to the Holy Land; they also discussed arrangements for the marriage of Louis's daughter Alice (who had been brought up at the English court since 1162) to Richard. In the following year Louis visited Canterbury to pray at the shrine of St Thomas for the recovery of his only son Philip from a dangerous fever. Henry joined him, presumably with mixed feelings.

In 1179 too, Richard was installed as duke of Aquitaine. His mother was taken from her prison and brought over to Aquitaine, where she publicly renounced the duchy in favour of her son. She then returned to England and captivity. It seems that for a short time—probably the only time—there was some ill feeling between Eleanor and Richard.

Some pitied the queen. The Benedictine Richard the Poitevin

wrote a moving lament for her: 'You have been ravished from your own country and carried off to an alien land', this faithful monk apostrophizes her, 'you enjoyed the pleasures of your ladies, their songs and the music of lute and tabor. And now you must grieve and weep and are eaten up with sorrow . . . You cry out but no one listens because it is the king of the north who holds you captive. Yet cry out still, unceasingly; raise your voice as if it were a trumpet and then it shall reach the ears of your sons. The day is coming when they will deliver you and when once more you shall dwell in your own land.' The monk puts words into Eleanor's mouth: 'Alas, my exile has been a long one. I have lived with a crude and ignorant tribe.' The words may well reflect the queen's true feelings about the English, as they obviously do those of many Aquitainians.

At the end of 1179 Louis VII was paralysed by a severe stroke and, after lingering for nearly a year, died in September 1180. There is no record of when Eleanor heard the news or whether she felt any emotion at the death of the husband with whom she had spent fifteen years. But in time to come she was certainly to rue the accession of the new king of the French, Philip II Augustus. For the moment, however, he was too young to seem a danger to anyone.

Meanwhile her sons were squabbling savagely. Some of the Poitevin lords had risen in support of the young king, whom they preferred to count Richard. One of the chief agitators was the famous troubadour baron, Bertran de Born, of whom a modern historian has written: 'In the person of this meteoric and malignant troubadour all the worst and best qualities of southern chivalry were blended.' Bertran, who could put nearly a thousand troops into the field out of his own resources, boasts openly in one of his songs that 'I am never happy unless the rich barons are at feud'. What made him particularly dangerous was his charm, to which all the Plantagenet princes were susceptible.

In 1182 the young king, accompanied by Geoffrey, invaded

Poitou, and a full-scale civil war broke out. Henry tried to make peace between his ferocious sons but they ignored him and the conflict continued. The young king had assembled an army of adventurers and mercenaries, who plundered far and wide, sacking abbeys and churches without a qualm. Peter of Blois wrote to the young man to accuse him of having become no more than 'a leader of freebooters', of consorting with 'outlaws and excommunicates'. But young Henry suddenly fell ill and found himself without resources. The few followers who remained faithful to him had not even enough money to buy food.

In June 1183 the captive queen had a most vivid dream. She saw her son, the young king, lying on a bed with his hands together, like some effigy on a tomb; there was a great, glowing sapphire ring on his finger, and on his head were two crowns: the first was the one that she had seen him wear, and the other was a circlet of heavenly light. Some days later the archdeacon of Wells came to her with the news that her eldest surviving son had died at Martel on 11 June. He had contracted dysentery and, realizing that he was mortally ill, had despatched a messenger to his father to beg his forgiveness; in reply the old king had sent him a sapphire ring as a token of reconciliation, and after his death it could not be removed from his finger. The archdeacon noted down Eleanor's dream, commenting that she had borne the sad news with much bravery and self-control because she had understood the meaning of her vision. She told him that, 'Eye hath not seen, nor ear heard, neither have entered into the heart of man, the things which God hath prepared for them that love Him'. Her imprisonment seems to have made her turn to religion.

We know that Eleanor mourned her handsome, charming son—years later, she wrote to the pope that she was still tortured by his memory. And Henry II, whom he had wronged so often and so cruelly, was plunged into deep misery. Something of the glamour and attraction of the younger Henry may be gathered from the anguish of his friend Bertran de Born. The troubadour composed a *planh* (lament) that goes, in Ezra Pound's rendering:

> If all the grief and woe and bitterness,
> All dolour, ill and every evil chance
> That ever came upon this grieving world
> Were set together they would seem but light
> Against the death of the young English king . . .
> That was most valiant 'mid all worthiest men.
> Gone is his body fine and amorous,
> Whence have we grief, discord and deepest sadness.

On his deathbed the young king had implored everyone present to intercede with his father for the release of his mother. Henry may well have been impressed by his son's dying words. Shortly afterwards, Eleanor's daughter Matilda and her turbulent husband Henry the Lion, duke of Saxony—in exile for his rebellion against the German emperor—were allowed to visit her at Old Sarum. In June 1184 Eleanor was permitted to go to Matilda's lying-in at Winchester, when she was presented with a grandson. The Pipe Rolls record the old king's gift to his estranged queen of a scarlet dress trimmed with grey miniver (weasel) and some embroidered cushions, together with rewards for her maid Amaria; far from being evidence of magnanimity, this may reflect the shameful poverty to which Henry had reduced her. Later that year she was given a fine gilt saddle. Then she was summoned by the king to keep Christmas—a festival that began on 30 November—with him at Windsor together with her beloved Richard (now heir to the throne) and John.

The queen's presence, however, should not be attributed to her husband's forgiveness. Probably he wanted her co-operation in a redistribution of his empire, as he wished to give a substantially larger share to John, his favourite son. It does not appear that Eleanor gave the king much assistance. Bishop Stubbs thought that although Henry 'occasionally indulged her with the

142

show of royal pomp and power, he never released her from confinement or forgave her'. But modern research tells a slightly different story. It really does seem that henceforward, by degrees, her confinement was considerably relaxed, even if archbishop Baldwin of Canterbury's plea for her release in the following year was not granted in every respect. She is known to have been with Henry in his French territories between May 1185 and April 1186.

Ever since the death of the young king, Eleanor must have been recognized by Henry II as potentially valuable in any dealings with his children. He had loved his eldest son deeply, despite all his rebellions and betrayals. He plainly felt very differently about Richard, although he clearly recognized his energy and ability; perhaps Richard hated him because of his treatment of Eleanor, and perhaps Henry knew it. None the less the old king respected the young duke and accepted him as his heir, although he foresaw that, like his elder brother, Richard would try to make himself independent. It was here that Eleanor, whether she wanted to or not, could help in bringing him to heel.

Yet at the same time it may not be altogether fanciful to discern a softening in Henry's attitude towards his faithless queen during the later years of his reign. Gerald of Wales says of Henry II that those 'whom he had once hated he rarely loved', but that those 'whom he had once loved he rarely regarded with hatred'.

After the late 1170s, the Angevin empire was almost a federation. Henry retained England and overall control, but his sons ruled the lands across the sea. The latter intrigued constantly with or against each other and frequently against their father. The situation became even worse after the young king's death. Henry wanted Richard, as his new heir, to move to Normandy and give Aquitaine to John. Richard refused. For all his savage treatment of its barons, he seems to have loved Aquitaine deeply. In any case, he obviously considered that the remote and barbarous lordship of Ireland was quite sufficient for John. Accordingly, John and Geoffrey invaded Poitou on their father's instructions, but were easily repulsed by their brother, an excellent soldier. Richard then came to England, to pay homage to his father and promise both obedience and hostages, but refused to give up Aquitaine. Eventually Henry forced him to return the duchy formally to his mother at Rouen during the Easter court of 1185. It was a clever move, as both Richard and the barons of Aquitaine had remained devoted to her. Even so, Richard continued to rule Aquitaine undisturbed until his father died and he was able to make sure that he could keep it for good. Meanwhile John was sent to Ireland to take possession of his lordship, and infuriated the chieftains by his arrogance and by such jokes as pulling their long beards.

In 1186 Geoffrey of Brittany died, either from a fever or by falling from his horse during a tournament. Unlike Richard, he was a small, dark-haired man. Gerald of Wales gives us a daunting portrait of him: 'One of the wisest of men, had he not been so ready to deceive others. His real nature had more of bitter aloes in it than honey; outwardly he had a ready flow of words, smoother than oil . . . he was a hypocrite, who could never be trusted and who had a marvellous gift for pretence and dissimulation.' Duke Geoffrey believed that it was his family's inheritance to hate each other and to do one another as much harm as possible. He lived up to this idea fully, and once ordered archers to shoot at his own father. He was also a ruthless plunderer of abbeys who personally sacked the rich shrine of Saint Martial and Saint Stephen of Grandmont. At the same time he possessed extraordinary personal magnetism; at his funeral his friend Philip of France, who was noted for his coldness, had to be forcibly prevented from jumping into the grave after him. Seven months after his death Geoffrey's widow, Constance, bore a posthumous son to whom she gave the name of one of her Breton people's heroes, Arthur.

The last years of Henry II's reign were sad ones, dominated by quarrels with his sons. Gerald of Wales tells us of a cruel legend about the old king (which took the fancy of the Elizabethan antiquary William Camden). 'It is said of this Henry that in a chamber at Windsor he caused to be painted an eagle with four birds whereof three of them all attacked the body of the old eagle. The fourth was scratching at the old eagle's eyes, and when it was asked of him what thing the picture should signify, it was answered by him, "This old eagle", said he, "is myself and these four eagles betoken my four sons which cease not to pursue my death and especially my youngest son John which now I love most shall most especially await and imagine my death".' But it is clear from Henry's behaviour that his children's enmity took him by surprise, again and again.

The new French king, Philip II, was a brilliant and ruthless politician who knew only too well how to exploit his neighbour's difficulties. First Philip demanded the return of the Vexin as a consequence of the death of the young king, who had held it only as his wife's dowry. He then complained about the delay in solemnizing the marriage between Richard and Philip's half-sister, Alice of France, knowing very well that Richard was reluctant to marry her; the reason, according to Gerald of Wales (who was probably right), was that the old king had seduced the girl during her long stay at his court. When Henry proposed that she should marry John instead and be duchess of Aquitaine, Philip slyly revealed the plan to Richard. The latter was so infuriated that he agreed to co-operate in the war against his father.

The campaign was abandoned, however, when terrible news arrived from Outremer. In July 1187 the army of the crusader states had been annihilated by Saladin at the Horns of Hattin; Jerusalem and the Holy Cross were now in infidel hands, and of all the Holy Land only two or three seaports remained to the Christians. The pope proclaimed a new crusade and the emperor, the kings of France and England and count Richard took the cross. Henry had been offered the crown of Jerusalem by the patriarch Heraclius in 1185, and had declined it. But now he and his sons may have had second thoughts: the current king, Guy of Lusignan, was hopelessly discredited. Henry began to assemble an expedition, imposing a savage tax—the Saladin tithe—to pay for it. Before he was able to set out, however, a new war began in France.

Richard was invading Toulouse. Count Raymond had tortured and murdered some merchants of Poitou, blinding and gelding them, apparently as a carefully considered insult. For all their friendship—they ate out of the same dish and slept in the same bed when they were together—Philip, as overlord of Toulouse, could not tolerate Richard's attack on his vassal. In June 1188 the French king struck in Berry, storming several castles. Henry immediately sailed from England with an army of Welsh mer-ceneries, while his son swung north and quickly expelled the French from Berry. The war spread to Normandy and Anjou. But, in a series of skilful diplomatic moves, Henry detached two of Philip's chief allies—the counts of Blois and Flanders—while the French king began to run out of money. By November it looked as though the Angevin had proved too much for the Capetian.

Then Richard turned against his father. He demanded that his marriage to the unfortunate Alice should take place at once (he was almost certainly insincere), that Henry should guaran-tee his succession to the throne of England, and that he should immediately be given full possession of Anjou, Maine and Tou-raine as well as Poitou. The old king refused all his demands. In his father's presence Richard thereupon formally declared him-self king Philip's vassal, kneeling swordless before him, placing his hands in his and doing homage to him for every Angevin fief in France. It was unfilial, even unnatural; consciously or unconsciously, Richard may have felt that in some way he was

146

avenging the wrongs that his father had inflicted on his adored mother. A truce prevented the war from breaking out again until Easter 1189, and the pope tried desperately to put an end to the quarrel, which could have wrecked his crusade.

In June 1189 the combined armies of count Richard and king Philip invaded Maine. In residence at the capital, Le Mans, Henry had too few troops to stop them. He set fire to Le Mans, although it had been his birthplace—some say that the burning was an accident—and fled towards Angers, pursued by his son. But Richard found his way barred by William Marshal, the most redoubtable knight of the age. Afraid for once, the count cried out, 'Marshal, don't kill me—it would be wicked as I'm unarmed'. William replied, 'I shan't kill you, but I hope the devil does', and drove his lance into Richard's horse to bring him crashing to the ground.

Shortly afterwards, Henry, who was seriously ill from blood poisoning, met his enemies at Villandry. Swaying in the saddle but refusing to dismount, he agreed to all their demands. As he gave his son the kiss of peace, he whispered in Richard's ear, 'God grant that I don't die before I can take my revenge on you'. But the old king had to return to Chinon in a litter, a dying man. He was so bitter that at first he refused to be shriven. 'Why should I revere Christ? Why should I honour Him who dishonours me?' For Henry had learnt on his deathbed that even his favourite child John had gone over to the enemy. Only his bastard son Geoffrey remained with him. His face turned to the wall, Henry II's last words were, 'Shame on a conquered king'. Eleanor had been revenged in full.

12 Queen Mother

'The eagle of the broken vow shall find joy in her third nestling.'

Geoffrey of Monmouth

'The king then sold everything that he had, castles, towns and manors.'

Roger of Howden

In his famous *Prophecies of Merlin*, Geoffrey of Monmouth had foretold how 'The eagle of the broken vow shall find joy in her third nestling' (*Aquila rupti foederis tertia nitidatione gaudebit*). Later the dean of St Paul's, Ralph of Diceto, was not slow in seeing that these words might be applied to the queen mother and Richard I. Eleanor was of course an imperial eagle, 'because she spread her wings over two kingdoms, those of France and England'; the broken vow signified both her divorce by king Louis and her imprisonment by king Henry; and the 'third nestling' was the new king, her third surviving son. The dean was not necessarily a sycophant in claiming that Eleanor found joy in Richard: everyone must have known that he was her favourite child.

On hearing that his father was dead, Richard came in a repentant mood to weep by the bier before the interment at Fontevrault. Then he seized the royal treasure at Chinon and sent orders to England for the release of his mother. His messenger was his erstwhile enemy, William Marshal. When William arrived at Winchester where Eleanor had been imprisoned, however, he found that she had already freed herself and was 'more the great lady than ever'. Her son had directed that she was to order everything as she wished and that her commands were to be obeyed implicitly. She at once gathered the court together, and went on progress 'from city to city and from castle to castle, just as she pleased'. That she was able to free herself so promptly is a revealing witness to the widespread recognition of the bond between herself and the new king; not even the justiciar dared to resist her. A modern French historian had described queen Eleanor as emerging from captivity transformed, 'a sovereign in full sail'.

Anxious to court popularity while establishing his rule, king Richard told his mother to release large numbers of prisoners. Accordingly, she sent an order throughout England for the freeing of men who had been unjustly imprisoned, notably for

151

infringing the tyrannical forest laws, or because of malicious ac-
cusations. When issuing the order Eleanor remarked that she
herself had found 'by her own experience that prisons were hateful to men, and to be released from them was a most delightful
refreshment to the spirit'. Another who benefited was her old
ally of 1173, Robert Beaumont, earl of Leicester, whose lands
were restored to him.

Strictly speaking, as in Henry's reign, the regent of England
was still the justiciar Ranulf Glanvill. But Richard was no friend
to Ranulf and during the five weeks before the new king's arrival
Eleanor was ruler of England in all but name. To a woman so
fond of power it must have been a most agreeable interlude. She
showed her mettle as an administrator, issuing edicts that stan-
dardized weights and measures for wheat and cloth throughout
the realm and established a single value for the coinage, putting
an end to regional variations in the price of silver from which
only bankers and moneylenders had profited. She freed the
abbeys of their obligation to stable or pasture herds of royal
horses, and founded a hospital in Surrey. Above all she ordered
'that every free man in the whole realm swear that he would bear
fealty to the lord Richard, lord of England and son of the lord
king Henry and the lady Eleanor, in life and limb and earthly
honour, as his liege lord, against all men and women living or
dead, and that they would be answerable to him and help him to
keep his peace and justice in all things'. She was also busy with
arrangements for the forthcoming coronation of her son.

After being acclaimed duke of Normandy, Richard sailed from
Barfleur and landed at Portsmouth on 13 August. Next day he
joined Eleanor at Winchester, and then mother and son rode to
Windsor and thence to London. Richard was crowned king of the
English in Westminster abbey on Sunday 3 September by archbishop Baldwin of Canterbury, in a ceremony very like that used
today. It seems to have been unusually splendid, to judge from
contemporary chronicles: the crown was so heavy that two earls

had to hold it over the king's head.

The coronation was followed by a banquet at which, according to the king's orders, no woman or Jew was present. One wonders if the ban applied to the king's mother. As for the Jews, some of their leaders tried to enter with gifts and, after being turned away, were set on by the mob; some of them were killed and a general massacre of Jews throughout London followed, much to Richard's irritation.

The new king was a very different man from his father, taking after Eleanor's family, the impetuous and eccentric Poitevin dynasty. The least English of all English sovereigns, his tastes were in many ways those of an Aquitainan robber baron; he was cruel and predatory, fond of battles and plunder, and happiest when on campaign. At the same time, he had a poetic streak and was a troubadour like his great-grandfather William IX. He also possessed his great-grandfather's love of display, which found expression in fantastic clothes. He was homosexual; and his mother was the only real love of his life. Even so, he did beget an illegitimate son, whom he wryly named Philip after his friend and enemy, the king of France. Indeed he had a rather odd sense of humour, together with a taste for the unexpected. He seems to have had small affection for England, which he had scarcely visited since his birth and of whose language he was totally ignorant; no doubt he winced at its uncouth Anglo-Norman French. Nevertheless the English cheered this tall and splendid new king with the red-gold hair. They knew nothing of his amorality and lack of scruple, of his sexual deviations, of his devotion to the weirder ideals of chivalry, of his reckless violence and brutality. Any change from Henry II's last oppresive days appeared an improvement.

It cannot be too much emphasized that Richard was devoted to his masterful mother, and Eleanor knew just how to control him. On his way to London he was informed that the Welsh had crossed the border and were raiding, burning and slaying. He announced that he would ride up at once and deal with them, but his mother ordered him to wait until he had been crowned, and he obeyed her. Later he not only restored her dowry in England but presented her with the dowries of the queens of Henry I and Stephen as well.

At sixty-seven Eleanor was remarkably well preserved, in an era when old age began at fifty. Not even the empress Matilda had reached such an age, yet Eleanor had another decade and a half of vigorous, active life ahead of her. Probably she appeared strangely young to her contemporaries. Régine Pernoud makes the point that the fashions of the period helped Eleanor to preserve a youthful image; the nun-like wimple hid white hair and a wrinkled neck. And no doubt she continued to paint her face, in the way that had once so scandalized St Bernard and the French clergy. We know from the Pipe Rolls that she took trouble with her wardrobe. At the time of the coronation she ordered a cape that consisted of seven yards of valuable silk edged with sable and squirrel (it cost over £4). She also ordered dresses of red cloth similarly trimmed. It is possible that she owed her longevity and her enduring energy and vitality to the enforced rest that she had taken during her fifteen years of imprisonment. But in any case she must have possessed a magnificent constitution.

To the disappointment of many, the new régime was very little different from that of king Henry. Richard retained all but a few of his father's officials, even those who had opposed him, including William Marshal. (The latter, who always told the truth, reminded the king that, 'I could have killed you, but I only killed your horse'.) Richard had no room for the adventurers who were his former companions; they were informed, with a certain irony, that traitors must not expect to be rewarded like honest men. The new chancellor was William Longchamp, bishop of Ely, a Norman of humble origins; and there was also a new justiciar, bishop Hugh Puiset of Durham. This was in no way a snub for Eleanor, who intended to accompany her son abroad. It is obvious that Richard wanted her to retain ultimate authority, to the point of over-ruling his ministers when necessary.

The new king also tried to make sure of his two surviving brothers. He loaded John with presents, giving him castles and estates all over England and marrying him to Isabella— sometimes called Hawisa or Avise—of Gloucester, who was the greatest heiress in the land. His illegitimate brother Geoffrey received the see of York, though not without opposition from its clergy; however, when Geoffrey failed to obtain possession of his archbishopric and (worse) the revenues that he had promised Richard, the king revoked the appointment in a fit of rage. Richard also forbade John and Geoffrey to return to England during the next three years without his express permission. Later and most unwisely he relented in John's case, apparently at Eleanor's request. The queen mother can have had no illusions about her youngest son's capacity for treachery, but perhaps she wanted him in the kingdom to ensure a smooth succession to the throne if his brother should be killed on crusade.

Richard was obsessed by his expedition to the Holy Land. His officials combed the English ports for ships. As his father's treasure—valued at 100,000 marks (£33,000)—was insufficient, everything was up for sale, 'castles, towns and manors' according to Roger of Howden. The king later joked, 'I would have sold London itself if I could have found a buyer'. Geoffrey had to pay £3000 for his archbishopric. Richard was too impatient to wait for tax receipts to come in and literally auctioned not only lands but offices, honours and privileges of every kind; even William Longchamp had to pay something for his chancellorship. For 10,000 marks, king William the Lion of Scotland was allowed to buy back the castles of Berwick and Roxburgh, which strategically were of vital importance, besides purchasing other concessions including the renunciation of all homage. Using papal letters, Richard extorted considerable sums of money from men who had sworn to go on crusade but changed their minds. Sherriffs were removed so that their offices could be offered for sale, and certain officials who had grown rich under Henry II found themselves facing crippling fines. Richard also hoped to plunder the Jews, but a false rumour spread that he had ordered a full-scale massacre, and his subjects forestalled him by slaughtering every Jew they could find, burning their bonds and stealing their property. To do him justice, the king deeply regretted the massacre; not only did it lose him a great deal of money, but the Jews had been under his personal protection and their murder was therefore an insult to the king.

So quickly did he amass funds that Richard's expedition was ready to sail by the spring of 1190. It is said that he had hired or requisitioned a fleet of one hundred vessels, from the Cinque Ports and other southern English harbours, and from Poitou and Normandy; among them was the *Esnecca*, the royal vessel that may have carried his mother to captivity fifteen years before. It has been estimated that the fleet provided transport for approximately 8000 men. The king himself preceded his armada, sailing from Dover on 11 December; he was ill and feverish, so that before he had even left England men said he would never return.

Almost as soon as Richard crossed to France, trouble broke out between the justiciar Hugh Puiset and the chancellor William Longchamp, each claiming to be the other's superior. The king held a council at Rouen on 2 February 1190 and later decided to make William Longchamp chief justiciar south of the Humber, while the north was to be under Hugh Puiset. Unfortunately, although their powers had been defined a little more clearly, there was still considerable ambiguity in their respective positions. Further unrest was inevitable.

In February the king's council was joined by that indispensable adviser, the queen mother. She brought with her poor Alice of France, Richard's betrothed, whom Eleanor was determined he should never marry. It was now that she unwisely persuaded Richard to release John from his oath to stay out of

England. As was customary, she endowed many abbeys and convents to pray for the success of the crusade and for her son's safe return. Among the beneficiaries were the Knights Hospitallers of the priory of France, who received the entire seaport of Le Perrot near La Rochelle, and her beloved nuns at Fontevrault. She took up residence at Chinon, where she had last been as her husband's prisoner: she was magnanimous enough to make a special endowment at Fontevrault for prayers 'for the repose of Henry's soul'.

Early in the summer of 1190 king Richard and king Philip met at Gisors to discuss the final details of their joint crusade. Philip insisted on discussing the position of his half-sister Alice, demanding that Richard should marry her before setting out on an expedition from which he might possibly never return. The English king stalled. He refused to surrender either Alice or her dowry, but argued that as women were not allowed to ride with their husbands on this crusade, the marriage must wait until he came home. Accordingly Alice remained in confinement at Rouen.

After saying goodbye to Eleanor at Chinon, Richard went to Tours, and finally set out on his crusade on 24 June 1190. The departure was not altogether happy, the crusaders weeping as they parted from their tearful families. There had been an ominous incident; when the English king received the insignia of a pilgrim—a staff and a flask—the staff broke in his hands. Nevertheless Richard went on to Vézelay (where half a century ago Louis and Eleanor had listened to St Bernard preaching the second crusade) and joined Philip. The joint armies marched at last on 3 July. Philip sailed from Genoa and Richard from Marseilles. The main English fleet had already left England, intending to join the king en route, but had been delayed by storms in the Bay of Biscay. He himself proceeded on a leisurely voyage down the west coast of Italy. When he reached Sicily he found his fleet waiting for him at Messina.

Richard was forced to stay longer in Sicily than he had expected. His brother-in-law William II had died in 1189, the last legitimate male of the royal house of Hauteville, and the throne had been seized by William's illegitimate cousin, count Tancred of Lecce. The latter's position was extremely insecure, as the legal heir was the formidable Henry of Hohenstaufen, the future emperor Henry VI, who had married an Hauteville princess. Tancred needed all his resources to maintain himself against this menacing claimant, so he refused to hand over to his predecessor's queen, Joanna, either her dowry or her legacy, and placed her in close confinement at Palermo. Richard was hardly the man to let his sister be treated in such a way. He immediately demanded her release, whereupon Tancred grew alarmed and sent her to him at Messina with some money, but still kept both the dowry and the legacy. The English king thereupon stormed one of Tancred's castles, which he gave to his sister to use as a dower house. Tancred was popular with his subjects, and fighting broke out between the English and the townsmen of Messina, which Richard then seized 'more quickly than a priest can say his matins'; he allowed his soldiers to sack the town thoroughly, announcing that he was going to keep it as a surety.

During this time Eleanor had not been idle, although she was now nearly seventy. By way of Bordeaux, she had ridden over the Pyrenees to Pamplona, the capital of king Sancho the Wise of Navarre. Here, on behalf of her son, she asked for the hand of Sancho's daughter Berengaria. Richard of Devizes tells us that Richard had met Berengaria during a tournament at Pamplona and infers that the king had been strongly attracted by her intellect. This may well mean that she had a taste for the *gai saber* and troubadours, in which case she was a princess after Eleanor's own heart. The chronicler also tells us ungallantly that Berengaria was more accomplished than beautiful. However, the match was probably Eleanor's idea. She wished to make sure that her son would never marry Alice of France. One can only guess at the reasons why the queen mother hated Alice so much: was it because she was her supplanter's daughter, or because she had been Henry's mistress, or did Eleanor fear a strong will that might threaten her own power?

Meanwhile Philip, who had now arrived in Sicily, was quarrelling once more with Richard about Alice. The French king pretended that he was angered at not having been given a half share of Messina, but the real reason was his half-sister; soon he and Richard were refusing to speak to each other. It was six months before Tancred gave way, paying Richard the vast sum of 40,000 bezants in gold, and betrothing his daughter to Richard's nephew and heir presumptive, the young Arthur, duke of Brittany, with a dowry of equal value. Richard mollified Philip by presenting him with a large part of the treasure that he had extorted from Tancred. The two monarchs wintered pleasantly in Sicily, though the Capetian chafed at both the delay and the expense. He sailed for the Holy Land as soon as possible, on 30 March 1191, and thus missed the arrival in Sicily of the English queen mother.

Eleanor and Berengaria had ridden over the Alps and all the way down the Italian peninsula to Brindisi. It was another daunting journey for such an old woman, yet she had undertaken it for the most statesman-like reason: she wanted to see that her favourite son not only repudiated Alice, but would marry a biddable princess and beget an heir. Richard himself may not have been over-interested. During his stay in Sicily he had knelt at a church door in Messina, bareheaded and naked save for his breeches, and publicly begged for absolution from his vices; four years later a saintly hermit was to reprove the king to his face for the sin of Sodom, to such effect that when he fell ill shortly afterwards he again did penance and recalled his wife to his side. Whatever his private feelings about marriage, however, Richard was too fond of his mother to go against her wishes. He sent a Sicilian ship to collect the two women, and rode across the

159

island to meet them at Reggio. They reached Messina on the very day that Philip of France set sail.

Eleanor's reunion with Richard—and also with Joanna, a child when she had last seen her, but now twenty-five—was a short one. As it was Lent, Berengaria's marriage could not be celebrated, but the king assured Eleanor that he would marry the princess as soon as possible, and the queen mother entrusted her future daughter-in-law to Joanna's care. Mother and son seem to have discussed problems of state: no doubt the distressing news that the English magnates were already quarrelling with the chancellor William Longchamp. Then on 2 April 1191, having spent only four days at Messina, Eleanor set off on the long journey home. A few days later Richard, accompanied by Joanna and Berengaria, sailed for Acre. His mother was not to see him again for nearly three years.

Escorted by the archbishop of Rouen (Walter of Coutances) and other great lords, Eleanor crossed the straits of Messina and rode up to Rome. She arrived there on Easter Sunday in the midst of the festivities for the coronation of the agreeably named Hyacinth Bobo (Giacinto Bobone) as pope Celestine III. The octogenarian pontiff was an old friend with whom she had been on good terms since he was in France in the early days of her first marriage, and also from a later period when he had benefited by her second husband's patronage. She had little difficulty in obtaining a legateship for the archbishop of Rouen, which if necessary she could use to bring William Longchamp to heel. She also extracted papal confirmation of the appointment of Geoffrey Plantagenet as archbishop of York, despite the opposition of William Longchamp and the English clergy. This was not generosity but shrewd politics: as archbishop he would finally abandon any thoughts of the crown, and he might prove a useful ally. Her only other business in Rome was to drive a hard bargain with the Roman moneylenders over her travelling expenses. She left the Eternal

City as quickly as possible, crossing the Alps and passing through Bourges on her way to take up residence at Rouen. It was almost exactly the same journey that she had made with Louis nearly forty-two years earlier.

In the meantime Richard's fleet was scattered by a storm off Cyprus. Some vessels were driven ashore and wrecked; they were plundered by the Cypriots, who imprisoned the survivors. The Cypriots also refused to allow Joanna and Berengaria's ship to shelter in Limassol harbour. Infuriated, Richard landed with his troops and in a matter of days had seized the entire island, together with its ruler, the self-styled 'emperor' Isaac Comnenus, whom he personally knocked off his horse and had placed in silver fetters (he had given his word not to put him in irons). He took the opportunity to marry Berengaria on 12 May in the Orthodox cathedral at Limassol, with much pomp. We do not know what Berengaria wore, but Richard appeared in a tunic of rose samite and a cape sewn with gold crescents and silver sunbursts, a scarlet cap decorated with gold beasts and birds, and cloth of gold buskins with gold spurs. The festivities lasted for three days.

Richard then left Cyprus (which he later sold to the Knights Templars), and reached Acre with his fleet on 8 June 1191. The crusaders besieging the great Palestinian seaport were saved from a disaster in the nick of time.

13 The Regent

'Eleanor, by the wrath of God, queen of the English.'

Eleanor's letter to pope Celestine III

'And who could be so savage or so cruel that this woman could not bend him to her wishes?'

Richard of Devizes on queen Eleanor

The next years show Eleanor at her most statesman-like. She had to defend Richard's possessions from the ruthless greed of his brother John and also against Philip of France, both of whom were determined to take full advantage of the king's absence, which proved unexpectedly long. But, in compensation, the queen mother possessed all the power she could desire, even if she was to know little peace.

Count John—so called from his county of Mortain in Normandy—knew very well that Arthur of Brittany was his brother's heir presumptive. He was therefore anxious to establish as strong a claim to the succession as possible, either to part of the Angevin empire or to the whole. Moreover he soon convinced himself that Richard would never return from the east, and he hoped to convince the people of England as well. Richard of Devizes informs us that the count travelled throughout the realm, 'making himself known, as Richard had never made himself', to people of all classes, installed his own garrisons in the royal castles, and circulated a rumour that Richard would never come back and that John was his heir.

The stupidity of the chancellor and senior justiciar, William Longchamp, provided just the sort of troubled waters that John wanted. Not only was William repellently arrogant but, intoxicated by his elevation, he did not bother to court popularity; the chroniclers noted grimly his favourite saying, that the fate he dreaded most was to turn into an Englishman, and recorded how his unwilling subjects mocked at his puny stature, 'snarling' ape-like face, hump back and lameness, and were constantly harping on the fact that his grandfather had been a serf. In addition it was widely believed that he was a pervert. His excessively splendid household and his lavish gifts of manors and offices, rich wardships and heiresses, to his relations particularly irritated the magnates. William had every intention of obeying Richard's orders to the letter, but he was without any political sense whatsoever.

When Geoffrey Plantagenet, armed with the papal confirmation given to him by Eleanor, tried to travel to England to claim his archbishopric of York, the chancellor gave orders that no port should allow him to land. When Geoffrey did land at Dover, in September 1191, he suffered the indignity of being arrested by William's sister Richeut, who was the castellan's wife. He tried to take sanctuary in a local Benedictine priory, but was pulled out by the legs and dragged through the mud to the castle, where he was thrown into a dungeon. To add insult to injury William confiscated Geoffrey's horses and had them brought to him as though they were 'spoils of war'.

William Longchamp had gone too far: both the English barons and the English prelates were outraged. The Carthusian bishop of Lincoln, St Hugh, who was certainly no politician and whose motives were always impeccable, promptly and publicly excommunicated the castellan of Dover and his wife for sacrilege. Geoffrey was quickly released, but by now count John had seen his opportunity and had called the magnates of the realm to a special council at Reading. They responded enthusiastically, summoning the chancellor to come and explain his disgraceful behaviour. On 6 October the bishops excommunicated him. William took refuge in the Tower of London, after vainly trying to persuade the citizens that John was trying to usurp his brother's throne. On 10 October in St Paul's, an assembly declared that William was deposed from his office. Eventually he surrendered and was allowed to take refuge in Dover Castle. He tried to escape across the Channel, disguised as an old woman, and was discovered when a fisherman tried to kiss him. But count John allowed the wretched man to leave England after all.

John did not benefit from the upheaval as much as he had hoped. He obtained possession of some of the royal castles, was recognized as his brother's heir, and was given the empty title of 'supreme governor of all the realm', but that was all. The English magnates were interested only in ridding themselves of

William Longchamp, not in replacing king Richard by his giddy and inexperienced brother. Instead there was a new justiciar: Walter of Coutances, archbishop of Rouen, who produced a specific mandate from Richard. One may detect Eleanor's shrewd hand in this appointment. She had almost certainly anticipated the crisis; the testimony is her extraction of that special legateship for Walter from the pope, and she had probably arranged the mandate as well.

There were also more dangerous matters to worry her. She was keeping Christmas at Bonneville-sur-Touques in Normandy when unexpected news came that king Philip was back from the Holy Land and was already at Fontainebleau. He had fallen dangerously ill from fever during the siege of Acre, losing all his hair, and had used his sickness as an excuse to be dispensed from his crusader's vow. He returned with the intention of exploiting his rival's absence as much as possible. He began at once to increase his garrisons on the Norman frontier and by 20 January 1192 was besieging Gisors. He also sent messages to count John, inviting him to visit the French court and offering him all the Plantagenet lands in France together with the hand of his ill-used half-sister, Alice. Unscrupulous as always, John immediately began to assemble an army at Southampton.

Eleanor took prompt action. All frontier garrisons in Normandy, Brittany, Anjou, Poitou and Aquitaine were put on the alert, their seneschals receiving exact orders. Philip was told firmly that to try to seize the property of a man on crusade was to break the 'truce of God': he reluctantly bowed to convention and retreated. Meanwhile the queen mother took ship and crossed the Channel on 11 February, before John could sail.

Richard of Devizes, a monk of Winchester, gives a glowing and even sentimental account of Eleanor's handling of the situation:

> Suspecting that this irresponsible young man might attempt some scheme, suggested by the French king, his mother grew anxious and

tried every possible means of stopping him from going abroad. Remembering the fate of her two elder sons, how both had died young before their time because of their many sins, her heart was sad and wounded. She was therefore determined, with every fibre of her being, to ensure that her younger sons stayed true to each other, so that their mother might die more happily than their father had done. . . . Through her tears and the pleading of the nobles of the land she managed with great difficulty to make him promise not to cross the Channel.

In reality, instead of wasting time arguing with John, Eleanor summoned the great council of the realm to meet at Windsor, at Oxford, at London, and at Winchester. With the unanimous support of the magnates, she and the chief justiciar forbade him to leave England and made it clear that if he did so he would forfeit all his English lands and revenues. For the moment at least, Philip and John were held in check.

Richard had been a glorious success in the Holy Land. In a few weeks he captured Acre, which had resisted the crusaders for two years, although on arrival he had immediately been struck down by a vicious local fever. He had high hopes of recapturing the entire Latin kingdom, where he stayed for over a year. On 7 September 1191 he won a magnificent victory on the plain before Arsuf, routing Saladin's cavalry. Unfortunately he delayed to refortify Jaffa, and when he eventually marched on Jerusalem in November, the winter rains ruined his campaign. The king then began to negotiate with Saladin. One interesting proposal was that his widowed sister Joanna should marry the sultan's brother Saphadin and that they should rule Palestine together as king and queen of Jerusalem, all Christians being allowed access to the Holy City. Richard even went so far as to knight Saphadin, but Joanna was horrified by the proposal and publicly refused to co-operate, on grounds of religion. In August 1192 Richard again managed to defeat Saladin, at Jaffa, but at once fell ill. In the end peace was reluctantly concluded for three

years, guaranteeing the towns reconquered by the crusaders and
allowing pilgrims limited access to Jerusalem. A king was found
for the realm that had been so miraculously saved from extinction, in the person of Eleanor's grandson, Henry of Champagne.
Richard finally left Palestine on 9 October 1192, having sent
Joanna and his wife before him to say that he meant to keep
Christmas in England. He left behind him a legend: a century
later Arab mothers were using the name of the warrior English
king to quieten their children, and horsemen spoke it to their
mounts to curb them.

The king had every reason to return home as quickly as possible. In April, letters had come from his mother to tell him of
Philip II's invasion of Normandy and of how John was plotting
to seize the throne. She had begged him to come as soon as he
could. It does not seem that she sent further letters to say how
successfully she had coped with these threats. If so, one can
hardly blame her: she wanted her favourite son back.

But Richard then disappeared, much to Eleanor's alarm.
Throughout England, prayers were offered and candles were lit
for his safety. Many people must have suspected that he had been
drowned at sea in some storm. It was known that his sister and
his wife had reached Brindisi safely and were on their way to
Rome. All that was known of the king's ship, the *Franche-Nef*—
which had sailed unescorted—was that it had put in at Cyprus
and Corfu and had then apparently made for Marseilles,
although another vessel that met it en route thought it was
bound for Brindisi. In fact the royal ship was blown back by a
storm towards Corfu. No news of the king had reached England
by Christmas; then, on 28 December, a messenger arrived from
the archbishop of Rouen with the amazing news that the duke of
Austria had arrested Richard somewhere near Vienna.

What had happened was a veritable Odyssey. After being
blown off course, Richard hired two Greek pirate ships as an
escort and sailed up the Adriatic. He put in at Ragusa but when

he continued his voyage he was caught in another storm and, after being driven past Pola, was wrecked on the coast of Friuli. He decided to continue overland, although he was in the territory of Mainard, count of Gortz, who was a vassal of the duke of Austria. Leopold of Austria was the sworn enemy of Richard, who had insulted him during the siege of Acre; when the duke had disobeyed the king's orders, Richard had had the banner of Austria thrown down and trodden into the mud. The English king disguised himself as 'Hugo, a merchant', and despite being recognized managed to evade capture for a while, but was eventually caught at the village of Ganina on the river Danube near Vienna; here he was arrested on 21 December in a common tavern, dressed as a cook and pretending to turn the spit. Duke Leopold imprisoned him in the hill-top castle of Dürnstein.

The young German emperor, Henry VI of Hohenstaufen, was a ferociously cruel and ruthless megalomaniac with dreams of universal empire, who would stop at very little in order to achieve his ambitions. He had good reasons for disliking the English king. First, Richard had allied himself with Tancred of Sicily, to which kingdom Henry was himself the legitimate heir. Second and worse, Richard was the brother-in-law and close friend of the leader of the Welf party, the pugnacious Henry of Saxony, who was the Hohenstaufen's most bitter foe. Henry therefore wrote with relish to Philip of France to inform him that Leopold had arrested 'the disturber of your realm, Richard, king of the English', having called to mind 'the treason, treachery and mischief of which he was guilty in the Promised Land'. Probably the emperor hoped that the prisoner might prove useful in bringing Philip to heel. In May 1193 Henry succeeded in forcing duke Leopold to hand over his precious captive, in return for a promise of part of the ransom, and incarcerated him at Speier.

As soon as Eleanor heard of Richard's arrest, she took control of affairs of state, although she did not formally adopt the title of regent. The man through and with whom she ruled was the new justiciar, the king's official deputy in the eyes of the law. This was her old aquaintance Walter of Coutances. A Cornishman despite his name, he was a typical career churchman of the period. He had been seal bearer to Henry II and treasurer of Rouen besides being archdeacon of Oxford and bishop of Lincoln. His appointment to the archbishopric of Rouen dated from 1184. It was Walter who had secretly begun the attack on William Longchamp in 1191, by persuading count John to rouse the English magnates. While helping to organize opposition to Longchamp behind the scenes, Walter pretended to remain his friend—Richard of Devizes roundly accuses him of double dealing. Then, when he had become justiciar in Longchamp's place, he immediately seized the latter's lands on behalf of the crown. In later years Walter would quarrel with king Richard over trivial matters, and in the next reign he would go over to Philip II. However, Eleanor had no difficulty in making use of the undoubted political and administrative talents of this greedy and rather devious cleric.

The queen mother also had the benefit of other excellent servants during her 'regency'. Of these the foremost was the extraordinarily able Hubert Walter, who later became justiciar himself as well as archbishop of Canterbury. A tall, handsome East Anglian, taciturn and apparently more than a little masterful in manner, Hubert Walter was the nephew of an earlier justiciar, Ranulf Glanvill, and according to his enthusiastic admirer bishop Stubbs, 'had been fitted by education to be a sound lawyer and financier as well as a good bishop and a successful general'. Hubert had begun his career as one of Henry II's chaplains and had since been a royal judge and a baron of the Exchequer. His merits were recognized and gained him the deanery of York and then the bishopric of Salisbury. He had accompanied Richard on the crusade as treasurer and his heroic efforts to help the sick and often starving rank and file during the siege of Acre made him extremely popular. Unfortunately he was still on his way back from the Holy Land and did not return to England until the spring of the following year. In later years he showed himself an administrator of genius who let 'the pressure of his master's hand lie as lightly as he could upon the people'. As flexible and accomodating as he was strong, Hubert would find no difficulty in working with the queen mother, who must have come to regard him as a tower of strength in those fearful days.

Another useful man was the Breton scholar Peter of Blois, archdeacon of Bath and later of London, who since 1191 had been acting—seemingly on a part-time basis—as Eleanor's chancellor or Latin secretary. It was a post of crucial importance, because all charters and letters were written in Latin. Peter was a person of considerable learning: so highly did contemporaries rate his professional skills that Henry II, a former employer, had had a collection made of his more historic letters. (Peter thought they were good too—Helen Waddell tells us that in one of them he 'modestly concludes that they will outlast ruin and flood and fire and the manifold procession of the centuries'.) He was a difficult creature—vain, pedantic and disappointed by lack of preferment—but the queen mother was able to make good use of his undoubted talents.

Although she now knew that her son was a captive, Eleanor had no idea where he was confined, or what were the plans of those who held him prisoner. She therefore sent the abbots of Boxley and Robertsbridge to Germany to search for the king, while the bishop of Bath went direct to the emperor to learn his intentions. There is no evidence for the romantic tale that Richard's favourite troubadour, Blondel, was the person who tracked him to Dürnstein and identified the king by his ability to join in a *tenso* (two-part song) that the minstrel sang from beneath the battlements, but it is quite in keeping with Richard's love of the fantastic.

Meanwhile the queen mother wrote terrible letters to the pope, drafted by that eloquent stylist, Peter of Blois. She complained furiously that the arrest of her son had violated the 'Truce of God', the hallowed convention that crusaders were free to come and go as they liked. She accused the pontiff of doing nothing to help when 'the kings and princes of this earth have conspired against my son, the Lord's annointed'. Richard 'is held in chains while another lays waste his lands . . . and all this while the sword of Peter stays in its scabbard'. She bemoans the young king and Geoffrey of Brittany who 'sleep in the dust' while 'their unhappy mother lives on, tortured by their memory'. In Richard, she continues, 'I have lost the staff of my age, the light of my eyes'. She even hints that she will bring about a schism and divide Christendom: 'The fateful moment draws near when the seamless robe of Christ shall be rent again, when St Peter's yoke shall be broken, when the Church shall be split asunder.' In one letter she calls herself 'Eleanor, by the wrath of God, queen of the English'. Despite this alarming correspondence Celestine III, who was now eighty-seven, was too old and timid to take swift action.

Understandably, Philip II and John were delighted by the news of Richard's misfortune and immediately began to exploit so golden an opportunity. The former seized Gisors and then besieged Rouen where, however, he was successfully defied by Eleanor's old friend, the earl of Leicester, who sarcastically invited the French king to come in and try his hospitality. But at last Philip had the Vexin. John crossed the Channel and summoned the barons of Normandy to meet him at Alençon and acknowledge him as his brother's heir. The summons fell on deaf ears, so he went to Paris, where he offered to do homage as duke of Normandy and duke of Aquitaine, and even as king of England, to confirm the surrender of the Vexin, and to divorce his wife and marry the unfortunate Alice of France. He then went back to England with an army of mercenaries, where he garrisoned Windsor and Wallingford, tried to occupy various other royal strongholds, and attempted to persuade the English barons to join him: he put it about that Richard would never return.

Eleanor's reaction to John's plotting was what one might expect from so shrewd a mother and so sophisticated a politician. Instead of confronting her youngest son, she simply out-manoeuvred him. She and the justiciars called out the English *fyrd* (home-guard). In the words of the chronicler: 'On the orders of queen Eleanor, who was then ruling England, in Passion week, at Easter and later, nobles and commons, knights and serfs, took up arms to guard the sea coast that faces Flanders.' Most of John's mercenaries were arrested as soon as they landed, and put in irons. John himself and a small party managed to reach England in secret and engaged a band of Welsh mercenaries. He and his supporters then established themselves at Windsor and at Wallingford. The queen's men at once besieged John in Windsor castle, besides investing all his other strongholds. Yet he might one day succeed to the throne after all, and Eleanor may have detected a certain nervousness in the English magnates. John held out stubbornly. Everything depended on how soon Richard would return to his kingdom.

In the meantime the two abbots had found Richard, in mid-March 1193, as he was being taken under escort to a new place of imprisonment on the Rhine. He cannot have been an easy prisoner: his chief relaxations were playing unpleasant practical jokes on his gaolers and trying to make them drunk. On 23 March the English king appeared before the imperial diet at Speier to defend himself against a variety of specious charges, after which he publicly exchanged the kiss of peace with the emperor. Henry was under strong pressure from the Welf (or anti-Hohenstaufen) magnates, who admired Richard, and also from pope Celestine, who had excommunicated duke Leopold for having violated the 'Truce of God' in seizing a crusader. The emperor was not going to overplay his hand, and he needed money badly. He was much too subtle to ill-treat or torture Richard in order to make him agree to a ransom: that would merely damage imperial prestige. Instead Henry simply threatened to hand him over to Philip of France.

On 20 April Hubert Walter at last returned to England. He had been in Sicily on his way home from the Holy Land when he heard of the king's arrest and had immediately gone to Germany to look for him. Having found Richard, he returned to his native land, bringing a depressing message from the king to the effect that to obtain his freedom he was probably going to need a ransom of 100,000 marks, though there was no guarantee that he would be set free on payment.

Then followed a letter from Richard, dated 19 April and addressed to 'his dearest mother Eleanor, queen of England, and his justiciars and all his faithful men in England', to say that William Longchamp—of all unlikely people—had persuaded the emperor to agree to see Richard at Hagenau after Hubert Walter's departure, and that king and emperor had made 'a mutual and indissoluble treaty of love'. Among other clauses this treaty stipulated that Richard was to pay a ransom of 100,000 marks and to provide military assistance for Henry's forthcoming campaign against Tancred of Sicily. The king asked his subjects to be generous in subscribing to the ransom and ordered some highly practical measures to be implemented. All Church plate of any value was to be impounded; every baron was to give hostages for his share, who would be under Eleanor's care before being sent to Germany; a register of the magnates' contributions was to be forwarded to Richard so that he might learn 'by what exact amount we are indebted to each one'. Significantly all monies were to be entrusted to the queen mother or to those nominated by her.

Eleanor and the two justiciars at once set about raising the ransom. It was a daunting task. The exorbitant sum mentioned in Richard's letter was confirmed in a 'golden bull' given by the emperor in person to William Longchamp, who in turn presented it to the great council of England when it met at St Albans in the first days of June 1193. Since April Eleanor had been trying to find the money, and by now she must have known that it would not be easy, because Richard had already bled the country white in financing his crusade. At the council she hopefully appointed officers to superintend the operation, and issued decrees for new taxes; these included one quarter of the yearly income of every man whether lay or cleric, a fee of twenty shillings—a vast amount for the period—from every knight, and, just as the king had ordered, the gold and silver plate from every church and abbey in the land; the Cistercian monks, the Gilbertine canons and the white canons, who possessed neither gold nor silver but owned enormous flocks of sheep, were to donate a whole year's wool-clip. Normandy and the other Angevin lands across the Channel were also burdened with these draconian levies. By Michaelmas, waggons were trundling down the muddy roads to London, laden with treasure that was to be placed in coffers at St Paul's cathedral under the seals of the queen mother and the chief justiciar.

In the event far less money was raised than the queen and the council had expected. Many people evaded the taxes or simply refused to pay them; abbot Samson of Bury St Edmunds threatened officials with the saint's curse if they dared to plunder his shrine. Despite the ruthlessness of the tax collectors a second levy and then a third had to be imposed. There was a good deal of administrative confusion; the money was not handled by the Exchequer, and the government had no clear idea of how much the new taxes and levies would bring in, so the collectors' accounts could not be audited properly. According to William of Newburgh, the collectors stole most of the money. It also seems that the actual tax-payers had few scruples about under-valuing their own resources.

Among those who exploited the confusion over taxes was count John, who levied them mercilessly in his own lands and estates and kept the money for himself. He still hoped that his brother would never return. However, early in July 1193 Philip of France received news that, because of fresh negotiations between the emperor and Richard, it seemed likely that the latter would be released before the end of the year. He immediately sent a warning to John: 'The devil has been let loose.' Terrified, the count slipped out of Windsor and fled from England to join Philip in Normandy. But even then John did not abandon all expectation of profiting in some way from his brother's captivity. He made a fresh alliance with the French king, offering him eastern Normandy and eastern Touraine if he would install him in Richard's possessions on the French side of the Channel; he also sent word to his supporters in England, ordering them to rise in revolt as soon as they heard that the French had invaded Normandy. However, Eleanor was ready. She had no trouble in persuading the great council to confiscate all John's English lands and to besiege his strongholds with more vigour than hitherto. Normandy proved equally loyal.

William Longchamp, the ousted chancellor and justiciar, had been causing the queen mother some concern. When he returned to England to deliver the emperor's bull and Richard's commands, he obviously had high hopes of re-establishing himself. But the bishops would not lift their excommunication, and London refused to admit him and barred its gates. At St Albans the great council treated him with public disdain and accepted the bull and the king's commands from him only after making him swear that he came simply as a bishop and a messenger, 'not as a justiciar, not as a legate, not as a chancellor'. Eleanor—as good a judge as ever of popular feeling—would not obey Richard's order that the young hostages be entrusted to Longchamp to take to Germany, and refused to hand over her grandson, thus enabling the magnates to disobey the king's command; they inferred that the man was a voracious homosexual, stating, 'We might put our daughters in his care, but never our sons'. It is probable that the queen mother complained about Longchamp to Richard, who soon recalled him.

The new negotiations between the emperor Henry and Richard that had so alarmed John and king Philip had taken place at Worms at the end of June 1193. After four days of wrangling, Henry and Richard reached a fresh agreement: the English king would be released on payment of 100,000 marks of the ransom money (the total was raised to 150,000 marks, 50,000 of this being instead of taking part in the expedition against Tancred of Sicily), and on receipt of 200 noble hostages as a guarantee for the remainder; the former 'emperor of Cyprus', still in his silver chains, was to be handed over to Henry; and Eleanor of Brittany, the daughter of Richard's brother Geoffrey, was to be betrothed to duke Leopold of Austria, the man who had captured Richard. When the imperial envoys came to London in October, Eleanor was able to show them that the necessary 100,000 silver marks were ready for shipment—thirty-five tons of precious metal.

Richard, understandably anxious that nothing should go wrong, sent orders that the queen mother should personally accompany the silver on its way to Germany. A fleet of vessels assembled at the Suffolk ports of Dunwich, Ipswich and Orford. It is very likely that Eleanor spent a night or two in the beautiful little castle at Orford; built by her husband in the 1170s, when it was the latest thing in military design, this elegant polygonal keep is one of the very few buildings in England that she would still recognize were she to return today. Accompanied by her faithful archbishop of Rouen, Walter of Coutances, by other great magnates (including William Longchamp), and by the 200 young hostages, Eleanor set sail with the treasure in December. Her fleet was packed with soldiers in case pirates should try to intercept so alluring a cargo. England was left in the capable hands of its new justiciar, Hubert Walter.

Despite the winter the queen mother seems to have had a smooth crossing. Once across the North Sea, she continued her journey by road and then up the river Rhine to join her son at Speier. Here she was to have celebrated the feast of the Epiphany (6 January) with him. But in the meantime the emperor Henry had postponed the date for Richard's release—originally intended to have been 17 January 1194—and was threatening to repudiate the precarious agreement between them. The exact reasons why Henry changed his mind will never be known. The most likely explanation is that it was because king Philip and count John were offering him a further 100,000 marks in silver if he would keep Richard in captivity until next Michaelmas, by which time they hoped to have partitioned his lands between them. Henry, who may have possessed a sense of humour, showed John's letter to Richard.

It must have been a cruel disappointment for Eleanor after her long journey in the depths of winter. She had not seen her favourite son since that short meeting in Sicily in the spring of 1191. But she quickly ended the deadlock in negotiations, with an inspired suggestion that showed all her skill as a diplomatist.

Plainly the emperor Henry, notoriously avaricious, had been strongly tempted by the prospect of more money from Philip and John. Indeed the latter was certain that the emperor would accept the offer and actually sent an agent to England to order his castellans to prepare for war. Henry, however, was alarmed at the outrage expressed by the princes of the empire; the king's imprisonment had been relaxed and he had employed his liberty to make useful friends among the Germans. Richard's charm and elegance had a considerable effect on the princes, who were already deeply impressed by his exploits in the Holy Land. (Probably he had even then begun to be known as 'the Lionheart', although it is unlikely that the legend of his tearing out with his bare hands the living heart of a lion that attacked him had yet developed.) Moreover Henry knew very well that Philip and John were hardly the most reliable of business partners. Then, in a public debate at Mainz before the princes, the English king aroused still more admiration by his majestic eloquence, calling on them to come to the help of a man who had been seized when on crusade. Many of his hearers shed tears.

The emperor realized that he would be wise to forgo Philip and John's bribe, but he wanted something else in compensation. To the consternation of the English he demanded that Richard should pay homage to him as his vassal. It was now that Eleanor intervened. Always a realist, she saw that by accepting this humiliating, though in fact meaningless condition, her son could escape. On her advice Richard took off his leather hat and placed it in the emperor Henry's hands as a sign of vassalage. The Hohenstaufen promptly returned it, stipulating that the English king should pay him a yearly tribute of £5000.

At long last, on 4 February 1194, Richard was released, 'restored to his mother and to freedom'. Those who witnessed Eleanor's reunion with her son wept at the spectacle. No doubt in her old age she could appear as pathetic as she was formidable. Indeed, in one of those frenzied letters to pope Celestine she had written of herself, with unaccustomed self-pity, as a woman 'worn to a skeleton, a mere bag of skin and bones, the blood gone from her veins, her very tears dried before they came into her eyes'. She and Richard then began a joyful progress together down the Rhine, via Cologne and Antwerp, where they were splendidly fêted. At Cologne the archbishop celebrated a Mass of thanksgiving in the cathedral; the introit began most fittingly, 'Now I know that the Lord hath sent His angel and snatched me from the hand of Herod', and every literate man present knew that this was not the introit for the day. At Antwerp they were the honoured guests of the duke of Louvain. Throughout the journey Richard took the opportunity of allying with as many local magnates as possible and especially with those lords in the Low Countries whose lands bordered the territory of the king of France.

Finally, on 4 March, Richard and Eleanor sailed from

Eleanor of Aquitaine and her daughter-in-law, Isabella of Angoulême: from a mural of about 1200 (discovered in 1964) in the Chapel of Sainte-Radegonde at Chinon. *Cliché Doloire.*

Fontevrault – the twelfth-century kitchen and refectory. *Photo Giraudon.*

Antwerp on board the *Trenchemer*. The royal admiral, Stephen of Turnham, who was commanding the little ship in person, had to employ experienced pilots to take her through the coastal islets and out into the estuary of the Scheldt. It was a long crossing, perhaps deliberately so, to avoid an ambush by Philip's ships, and the *Trenchemer* was escorted by a large and redoubtable cog from the Cinque port of Rye. Richard and his mother landed at Sandwich on Sunday 13 March 1194. The king had been out of his kingdom for more than four years. It was the end of Eleanor's regency in all but name.

14 Richard's Return

'Odysseus hath come, and hath got him to his own house.'

Homer, *The Odyssey*

'When his return from his long captivity had become an event rather wished than hoped for by his despairing subjects.'

Sir Walter Scott, *Ivanhoe*

It was about nine o'clock in the morning when Richard and Eleanor sailed into Sandwich. The sun shone with such a wonderful red glow that men later said they had known that it announced the return of the king. He and his mother did not linger at Sandwich but rode straight to Canterbury, where they heard the monks sing Sunday mass and Richard prayed at the shrine of St Thomas in thanksgiving.

William of Newburgh, who remembered Richard's return, wrote how, 'The news of the coming of the king, so long and so desperately awaited, flew faster than the north wind'. Everyone was weary of insecure government, of the threat of being ruled by a man as giddy and feckless as count John. Yet not all rejoiced. One of John's supporters, the castellan of St Michael's Mount, actually died of fright on hearing the news. Most people were deliriously happy however, and folk memory seems to have preserved something of their happiness in the legend of Robin Hood. Perhaps Sir Walter Scott's *Ivanhoe* is not so very far from the truth after all.

London prepared a magnificent reception for Richard,

> Richard that robb'd the lion of his heart,
> And fought the holy wars in Palestine.

The streets were decked with tapestries and green boughs. Ralph of Diceto, the dean of St Paul's, who was almost certainly present, tells us that the king was 'hailed with joy in the Strand'. In the city Richard was escorted by cheering crowds to St Paul's, to be welcomed at the cathedral by a great throng of clergy. Some of the emperor's German officials, in London to collect the remainder of the king's ransom, were astonished by the general rejoicing and by the city's obvious prosperity; they grumbled sourly that they had expected London to have been reduced to utter poverty from paying the money demanded by their master, and that had he realized how rich the country was, he would have asked for much more—the lamentations of the English had deceived him.

Richard then rode to the shrine of the martyred East Anglian king, St Edmund, at Bury St Edmunds, to give thanks to the man who appears to have been his favourite saint. Then he went to Nottingham. It was time for him to restore complete order in England and to deal with his brother John's supporters.

Nottingham, one of John's castles, was still holding out for its master, as was Tickhill in Northumberland, which had just been invested by the bishop of Durham. The two garrisons believed John's lies and could not credit that the king had returned. When two of the knights inside Nottingham came out and saw that it really was Richard who was beseiging them, however, the castle surrendered at once, on 27 March. Tickhill had fallen a few days earlier and count John's revolt was now completely crushed. In the ensuing great council at Nottingham—at which the queen mother was present—the king summoned his brother to appear before it within forty days or forfeit any right to succeed him in any of his territories. At the same time pope Celestine responded tardily to Eleanor's appeals, and excommunicated both John and Philip of France for violating the 'Truce of God'.

Meanwhile, on Low Sunday 17 April 1194, Richard was re-crowned at Winchester by archbishop Hubert Walter of Canterbury. Eleanor sat in the north transept of the cathedral on a special dais, surrounded by great ladies as though in one of her courts of love. She had been a good steward for her son; in bishop Stubb's words: 'Had it not been for her governing skill while Richard was in Palestine, and her influence on the continent . . . England would have been a prey to anarchy, and Normandy lost to the house of Anjou long before it was.' Even if she herself was not re-crowned during the splendid ceremony, she sat there as queen of the English. Perhaps significantly, Berengaria was not present, but was far away in Poitou—no doubt to Eleanor's complete satisfaction.

Despite the loyalty of the English, king Richard was anxious to return to his lands across the Channel, which he still loved best. After only a few weeks in England, having imposed even harsher taxes and sold yet more offices of state, he summoned his English knights—as many as one in every three—to follow him to France. On 22 April he left Winchester for Portsmouth, where he and his mother took ship, but only to be blown back by a fearful storm. Eventually it abated and on 12 May they were able to sail, with their fleet of one hundred vessels. The king had left England for the last time, although he was to reign for another five years. Nor would Eleanor herself ever return to England.

The royal couple landed at Barfleur, to receive the same ecstatic welcome from the Normans that they had been given by the English. Their progress through Normandy took them to Caen and Bayeux and then to Lisieux. At Lisieux they went to the house of the archdeacon, John of Alençon, to spend the night. That evening, much to his embarrassment, the archdeacon was informed by a servant that count John was waiting at his door 'in a state of abject penitence'.

Philip of France had no use for ruined allies who had lost their lands, and the count had been brought very low. The prodigal son hoped that his mother might at least temper the wrath of his brother. The archdeacon went into Richard's chamber, where the king was resting before supper, but was too nervous to speak. However Richard at once guessed that John was outside. 'I know you have seen my brother', he said; 'he is wrong to be afraid—let him come in, without fear. After all, he is my brother.' John entered, threw himself on the ground and crawled to the king's feet, begging for forgiveness. 'You are a mere child', said Richard; 'you have been ill advised and your counsellors shall pay for it.' There was clearly an element of contempt in the king's magnanimity: the 'child' was nearly thirty. Nevertheless Richard produced a fatted calf, in the shape of an enormous salmon that had just been presented to him by some loyal

Norman, and ordered it to be cooked, telling John to make a good meal. The following year he gave him back Ireland, together with his county of Mortain and earldom of Gloucester, and also his honour of Eye. For the rest of the reign John remained loyal. In fact he owed his miraculous pardon to his mother: Roger of Howden makes it perfectly clear that it was due entirely to Eleanor's pleading. As will be seen, her motives cannot have been wholly maternal.

Richard wanted to return to the Holy Land as soon as possible. Unfortunately Philip II's determination to destroy the Angevin empire made it out of the question, and the king had to spend the rest of his life in almost unceasing frontier warfare with the French. Eleanor was by now too old and infirm to take part in these campaigns, as she might well have done had she been younger. Nevertheless, she must have had full confidence that Richard, who had the reputation of being the best soldier in western Europe, would prove more than a match for Philip of France.

Nor was her confidence misplaced. In June Richard hurled Philip out of Normandy, pursuing the French king with such speed that he had to hide in a roadside church. At the same time Richard restored order in Aquitaine, committing his usual atrocities when punishing rebellious barons, and also recovered eastern Touraine. Even if he did not regain all the territories that John had surrendered to the French, he had good reason for satisfaction when he concluded a twelve-month truce with Philip in November 1194.

John was by now fighting for his brother with enthusiasm. In May at Evreux he had 300 prisoners decapitated and stuck their heads on stakes around the citadel in a vain attempt to frighten it into surrender. Even king Richard was horrified, and rebuked the count.

The following summer the king's former gaoler, the emperor Henry, proposed an alliance with Richard and sent him a golden crown as a token of his sincerity. He hoped to make France a vassal state of the empire and was considering a joint Anglo-German invasion. Hearing of these moves, Philip invaded Normandy once again. A meeting at Vaudreuil between the two kings ended in uproar when Philip accused Richard of breaking his word; the latter was so angry that he chased the Capetian for some miles. In the autumn Philip took Dieppe, burning the port and the English shipping in the harbour; Richard succeeded in capturing Issoudun in Berry. A new peace was then made, giving Philip the Vexin and the Auvergne, but Richard kept his gains.

One beneficiary from the peace negotiations during 1196 was Richard's former betrothed, Alice of France, who was still unmarried at thirty-three in an era when royal princesses usually became brides at twelve or thirteen. She had been moved from her prison at Rouen to various castles, in case of any attempt at rescue. Her half-brother Philip, moved by considerations of strategy rather than affection, at last obtained her release and married her to count William of Ponthieu, whose county lay between Flanders and the northern Plantagenet lands; he was a usefully placed ally should king Richard and Baldwin of Flanders try to join forces. But at least Alice had acquired a husband whose rank was worthy of her. One cannot but suspect that Eleanor's withdrawal from affairs of state at this time had saved Alice from perpetual imprisonment.

A marriage of which Eleanor almost certainly knew and approved in advance was that of her daughter Joanna, the widowed queen of Sicily. Toulouse had always evaded the Plantagenets, but its acquisition meant the completion of their French empire. Eleanor had some claim to be considered its rightful heiress, and long ago both her husbands had claimed it in her name. Raymond VI, who succeeded his father in 1195, was not a very promising husband. He had already been married several times and was excommunicated for abandoning one wife to take another. Now Richard persuaded him to take Joanna as his fourth bride, giving her Agen for her dowry. It was not a happy match, but little could be expected from a man so unchristian as to incarcerate a previous spouse in a house of Albigensian *perfecti*, a Manichaean monastery where strict austerities were practised. Raymond himself was far from austere, and kept a harem. Nevertheless Joanna bore him a son and heir, the future Raymond VII (who would one day be the victim of the Albigensian crusade, a holocaust that was to destroy Provençal civilization and the troubadours). Even so, Toulouse was a valuable ally.

Probably the question that continued to worry Eleanor after Richard's return was the succession. She appears to have developed an intense dislike for the duchess Constance, mother of the heir presumptive, Arthur of Brittany. The duchess was very different from even a northern Frenchwoman, though French was no doubt her first language; most of her Breton subjects still spoke their Celtic tongue. Her marriage to Geoffrey Plantagenet can hardly have been particularly happy in view of his sour, twisted nature, but Constance was to experience worse. When Geoffrey died, Henry II married her off to earl Ranulf of Chester, who promptly took the title of duke of Brittany, only to be chased out of the duchy by the Bretons after the old king died. In 1196, when Constance was on her way to Richard's court, Ranulf seized her and imprisoned her in one of his castles. Eventually the couple reached some sort of agreement, but later they fell out again and there was a divorce in 1199; it was rumoured that the earl had been infuriated by count John's lustful advances to her. Eleanor's distaste for the duchess may be attributable to the fact that if Arthur succeeded, Constance, who was regent of Brittany, might reasonably expect to become regent of England and the entire Angevin empire as well; but there was almost certainly a personal element in her antagonism.

It would be interesting to know more about Constance, but the chronicles tell us very little. She may well have been a woman of the same forceful stamp as Eleanor herself, for Constance too was an heiress who lost her inheritance through marriage and regained it through her son. Shakespeare's characterization of her is astonishingly plausible, although it is based only on Holinshed's muddled reading of unreliable chronicles. In *King John* he portrays a mother trying desperately to save her child from implacable enemies. We can be sure that 'ambitious Constance' recognized that Arthur's very existence was a threat both to John and to Eleanor.

The queen mother looked for an alternative heir. Revealingly, she ignored John, although he was her own son; plainly she knew him too well to trust him. Her choice fell on another grandson, Otto of Brunswick, Matilda's child. In the spring of 1196, with Richard's approval, he was made duke of Aquitaine. Indeed Otto may have been promised the succession to the Angevin empire in its entirety, including England. But Otto disqualified himself by being elected emperor. Eleanor had every reason to hope that Richard might live for many years yet, however—perhaps until long after she herself was dead.

By the late 1190s it seemed that Eleanor's trust in her favourite son had been justified. Admittedly he was living apart from Berengaria, who appears to have been made to live away from the court on her estates in Maine, but at least Eleanor had no cause for jealousy. Chroniclers testify to the fact that Richard was becoming positively respectable. He heard Mass each day with commendable devotion (although he would not take communion, from scruples over his hatred for king Philip), gave alms to the poor, treated the clergy with respect, and even began to restore the church plate seized to help pay for his ransom.

Nevertheless, it has to be admitted that he retained the same cynicism about churchmen displayed by his mother in her prime. When the preacher Fulk of Neuilly accused him of begetting three shameless daughters, Pride, Avarice and Sensuality, Richard was ready with a retort worthy of William IX: 'I give my daughter Pride to the Knights Templars, my daughter Avarice to the Cistercians, and my daughter Sensuality to the princes of the Church.' No story illustrates more vividly how much he was a son after Eleanor's heart, but, like her, he was no persecutor of clerics.

Richard—'great one', as she called him—was exactly the heir the queen mother wanted. With his gifts as a soldier and a statesman, he appeared certain to defeat Philip of France and to perpetuate the Angevin empire. But Eleanor now watched from a distance.

15 Fontevrault

'Divine inspiration made me wish to visit the holy convent of the nuns of Fontevrault.'

A charter of queen Eleanor

'O God, O my God, hear me also a widow.'

The Book of Judith

The foremost authority on Eleanor's letters and charters, Dr Richardson, has shown that there is little documentary trace of her life between June 1194 and April 1199. In fact she had retired to her favourite religious house, the abbey of Fontevrault, near Chinon on the borders of Touraine and Anjou. Here she had come in moments of peace during the past, and now she returned, instead of going back to Poitiers. Here she plainly hoped to die. Her relationship with Fontevrault, on the banks of the river Vienne, reveals an unexpected and attractive side to the queen mother. It is the key to much of her personality in middle and old age.

The abbey had come into being almost by accident. Towards the end of the eleventh century a wandering preacher from Britanny, Robert of Arbrissel, established a little community on a patch of land near a fountain—i.e. Fontevrault—building huts and a chapel. Men and women lived apart, the former cultivating the land, the latter leading a life of contemplative prayer. Meanwhile Robert himself continued his wandering and preaching, mainly in Anjou and Poitou. His chief concern was to be 'above all a guide and a comfort to all who were desolate or who had gone astray', according to his earliest biographer, Baudry of Bourgueil. Robert was such an attractive personality and his sermons were so inspiring that he drew more and more people to his community, especially 'the poor, the sick, the incestuous, concubines, lepers, the weak and the aged'. It was a time when many new monastic orders were emerging. What made Fontevrault unusual was the number of women who joined it.

Robert did not care where they came from. At Rouen he converted an entire brothel whose inmates followed him home. So large did his community become that he had to divide it, setting up other settlements. Fontevrault itself contained 300 women, as well as the men. Robert found many rich benefactors and was therefore able to build a great abbey at Fontevrault and dependent priories. He gave his flock a rule based on that of St

Benedict, but with startling innovations. Each house was to be a double community of men and women—monks, lay brethren and nuns—although Robert regarded the latter as the most important. The head of the new order was to be a nun, the abbess of Fontevrault. She had to be a widow, because widows were both chaste and maternal and were accustomed to handling people and to running houses and managing property. The heads of the priories were also to be nuns. The rule made the monks and lay brothers completely subject to the abbess and her prioresses.

When Robert lay dying in 1116 he said: 'What I have built, I built for the sake of the nuns. I gave everything for them—my life, my ministry and my disciples.' He wanted to help all female victims of society, especially those who had been ill treated by men. Moreover he wished to provide a refuge not only for poor women and prostitutes, but for great ladies as well. In his day, marriage to a high-born woman was the quickest way to rank and fortune and the surest means of building a dynasty, as queen Eleanor knew only too well. Men married heiresses and then cast them off to marry richer ones, which was why so many marriages were within forbidden degrees of consanguinity, which could be used later as grounds for divorce. And wives had no redress or escape if their husbands beat them or installed concubines.

From the beginning, Robert separated his nuns into separate groups—lepers and prostitutes obviously required different treatment. The ladies, too, lived apart. They could become nuns, bringing their maids to be lay sisters, or they could simply live in the abbey in their own apartments; in either case they were able to retain something of their rank and status. In the words of a modern American historian, Amy Kelly, at Fontevrault 'the hierarchies of the world were there respected, the commitment dowries regal, the dignities high, the preferments honourable'. In addition Robert ensured that the abbey should enjoy the highest social prestige and wield considerable influence by insisting that the abbess herself should belong to some great noble family.

Orford Castle in Suffolk, one of the few secular buildings to remain much as
it was in Eleanor's time. *A. S. Kersting*.

Eleanor's youngest son, king John: from the effigy in Worcester Cathedral. *A. S. Kersting.*

Indeed the second abbess was no less a personage than Matilda of Anjou, widow of William Atheling, the son of king Henry I of England, who had been drowned in the White Ship. Eleanor, who came to know her well, refers to her in documents as 'my aunt'.

Battered and ill-used wives from all over France flocked to this haven where they could recover their self-respect and dignity. Here they found sympathy and spiritual comfort. Among them were the two wives of Eleanor's grandfather, William IX, who fled to Fontevrault because of his outrageous behaviour. Another was Bertrada of Montfort, countess of Anjou and mistress of king Philip of France (the grandfather of Louis VII), who became a nun there and died from her austerities.

The new order's contribution was revolutionary in an age that had hitherto regarded women as being almost as evil as the devil himself; St Bernard once wrote that 'to live with a woman without danger is more difficult than raising the dead to life', and regarded noblewomen as the worst of all; he actually called his own sister 'a clod of dung'. One has only to look at the serpentine temptresses of Romanesque carvings to realize how widespread was this fear and disgusted contempt among pious Christians of the period. In contrast Fontevrault consciously appealed to the scriptural example of the Virgin Mary and St John who took her into his house in obedience to the words of Jesus from the cross: 'Woman, behold thy son!' and, to John, 'Behold thy mother.' Symbolically, the churches of the order's nuns were always dedicated to Our Lady and the oratories of the order's monks to St John.

Even in the twelfth century Fontevrault was widely recognized as playing an important part in improving the status of women and in defending their rights. Its whole inspiration publicly proclaimed their individuality and their value as human beings. Indeed the abbess or *domina* was probably intended by Robert to provide a religious counterpart to the lady or *domna* of the troubadours. Hitherto even mistresses had been seen as no more than sexual objects. Some literary historians (e.g. Reto Bezzola) credit no less cynical a hedonist than William IX with being converted to a new concept of womanhood by the example of Fontevrault; his early verse is sensual to the point of grossness, but in a later poem he has discovered the fascination of an unattainable Beatrice, too exalted to be possessed.

Understandably, the order of Fontevrault became extremely popular. Ultimately it possessed one hundred dependent priories in France, together with three in England, which owed their foundation to Eleanor's encouragement. Most of their nuns came from aristocratic families. Even in the eighteenth century Louis XV sent his daughters to Fontevrault to be educated. As Miss Kelly says, the mother abbey was an asylum for 'ladies of rank whose worldly destinies were at an end, or the turbulent or merely inconvenient relics of kings and princes and high barons, or the superfluity of princesses that embarrassed noble houses'.

The ideals that inspired Fontevrault must have appealed deeply to Eleanor after her own experience of men. She too had been exploited and cast off. She had many friends and relatives among the nuns and would have known all about the abbey and its concept of a new and independent woman from a very early age. As has been seen, she endowed it as early as 1146, before she went on crusade.

Furthermore, despite the frivolity of her early years and the misgivings of St Bernard and certain chroniclers, Eleanor was undoubtedly a devout Christian. It was not just that she approved of Fontevrault as a haven for her sex. She was plainly impressed by the fervency of its nuns and monks, by the discipline of its two strictly segregated cloisters; a monk could not enter the cloister of the nuns even to give a dying woman the last sacraments, and to be annointed she had to be carried into the abbey church. It is clear that Eleanor placed a high value on the prayers of the community.

In 1168, when her son John was only one year old, she entrusted him to Fontevrault to be brought up by the nuns. It was probably at her instigation that Henry II endowed the abbey so generously. Fontevrault appears to have become one of his own favourite religious houses, and indeed he was to be buried there.

From 1152 onwards Eleanor herself gave Fontevrault some new gift at almost every crisis or important event of her life. In that year, immediately after her marriage to Henry, she declared in a charter: 'Divine inspiration made me wish to visit the holy convent of the nuns of Fontevrault, and by God's grace I have been able to do so. God has brought me to Fontevrault. I have crossed the threshold of the sisters and there, with deep emotion, I have approved, conceded and confirmed everything that my father and my forebears have ever given to the church of Fontevrault.' In 1170, when Richard was consecrated count of Poitiers, she endowed the abbey, and again in 1185 (perhaps to mark her partial reconciliation with Henry). She did so yet again in 1199, on the same day that her son was buried there, asking the nuns to pray for 'the soul of her very dear lord, king Richard'.

Furthermore, during that unhappy year of 1199, one of her own daughters became a nun at Fontevrault. This was Joanna of Toulouse, who was worn out by the infidelities of count Raymond and by the rebellions of his turbulent subjects. Attempts to dissuade the countess were in vain, although she was pregnant. She was so ill that she could scarcely take her vows, and she soon died. Her child was born posthumously, but it also died. The queen mother buried them in the abbey.

Eleanor herself had entered Fontevrault in 1194, shortly after king Richard's return from captivity, though not as a nun. Presumably it was able to offer her suitably regal accommodation; most great abbeys of the period were accustomed to entertaining royal guests. Moreover it was 'an excellent listening post', being near Chinon, which was the administrative centre of Touraine and Anjou and in the heart of the Angevin empire in France. From here she could easily keep an eye on the political situation and supervise her seneschals, castellans and stewards. Protected from the exhausting demands of public life, she could hold a quiet and intimate female court; by now she probably had little interest in men apart from Richard, who was often at Chinon and could come to see her frequently. The queen mother seems to have been on close terms with all the abbesses. Above all, it was an excellent place for an aged lady to prepare her soul for death. Occasionally she emerged, but she always returned to this last home.

At the Revolution the abbey was sacked, and the bones of the Plantagenets were dug up and scattered, and the building was turned into a prison. In the 1960s, however, the prisoners were removed from Fontevrault so that a thorough restoration could be made. It is a rambling complex of buildings, part of which dates from the sixteenth century or later, and much of it is undistinguished. But even today Eleanor would recognize the church and the kitchen. The first is a glorious Romanesque temple, consecrated in 1119, with a high and truly regal nave flanked by magnificent columns and lit by four great cupolas. The kitchen is one of the strangest edifices to survive from the twelfth century. In shape it is a double octagon, crowned by a vast central chimney surrounded by twenty lesser chimneys. The size gives some idea of how enormous the abbey must have been in its prime: this kitchen provided food not only for the community but for guests and travellers as well, sometimes feeding nearly a thousand people.

16 The Death of Richard

'A voice was heard in Rama, lamentation and bitter weeping; Rachel weeping for her children refused to be comforted for her children because they were not.'

The Book of the Prophet Jeremiah

'With the life of a generous, but rash and romantic monarch, perished all the projects which his ambition and generosity had formed.'

Sir Walter Scott, *Ivanhoe*

Philip II—sometimes called Augustus because he was born in August—was unquestionably one of France's most energetic and successful rulers. Like so many of her great kings, he was unattractive. Crafty, avaricious, suspicious, timid to the point of cowardice, he was totally lacking in the chivalry of Richard, and indeed in any ideals at all. He was a poor soldier, and could not even ride a horse properly. He had no time for music or troubadours. He looked like a peasant instead of a king, being short and squat, with a red face and tangled hair, and was unkempt and dirty in his person. No man could have been more different from Richard. Yet King Philip was also a supreme realist, with a true Frenchman's practicality, who knew just how to play the tortoise to the Plantagenet hare. His sole aim was to increase the Capetian domain, and he concentrated on this with fanatical determination. Even the most desperate reverse could not deter him. He was the most formidable enemy Eleanor ever knew, and in the end the son of the husband who had rejected her would win the battle.

Yet by the middle of the 1190s Richard appeared to have everything on his side. His alliances, with the counts of Flanders, Boulogne, Hainault and Toulouse and even with the emperor, hemmed in Philip. Moreover Normandy and Aquitaine, now at peace, provided rich revenues to pay for war. The symbol of Richard's military might was the impressive castle of Château-Gaillard, on a high cliff above the right bank of the river Seine—the 'rock of Andelys'—which he built during 1196, perhaps inspired by the mountain-top stronghold in which he had been incarcerated in Germany, or by the great castles of the Holy Land. Its name meant 'saucy castle' and its very existence was an affront, as well as an obstacle, to the French King and his ambitions. It blocked the approaches to Rouen, fairly and squarely. Philip was appalled when he first saw it, but joked bravely, 'If its walls were made of iron, I would still storm them'. Richard's reply, very much in character, was 'By God's throat, if its walls were built of butter, I would still hold them'. It became his administrative as well as his strategic centre, the emblem of the Angevin empire in France.

War between the two kings began once more in 1197. Philip managed to take Aumâle, but Richard made substantial gains. He was employing mercenaries and paid professionals, who more or less constituted a standing army. They included such technical experts as Ivo the Crossbowman (*Balestarius*)—the crossbow was the new weapon of the moment—and men he had brought back from the Holy Land who knew how to use Greek Fire (naptha) in primitive flamethrowers. Nor were his other mercenary troops to be despised, even if they were recruited from outlaws, bandits and renegade monks. Many came from Flanders and Brabant, and the popular nickname for them was 'Brabançons'. They had some excellent commanders, such as the ferocious Mercadier from Périgord.

In May count John captured king Philip's cousin, Philip of Dreux, the fighting bishop of Beauvais, and Richard advanced steadily in the Auvergne. In August Philip had to retreat ignominiously after trying to relieve Arras, which was beseiged by the count of Flanders. Indeed, far from coming to the French king's help, the great French feudatories had either begun to ally with Richard or else stood aside. Philip hastily made peace. His domains had suffered fearfully from the ravages of Mercadier, whose terrible mercenaries had burnt, murdered and plundered far and wide, sparing neither churches nor priests.

War broke out yet again in 1198, on the Norman frontier. Near Gisors Richard inflicted an all-but-decisive defeat on Philip, in the course of which he personally unhorsed three French knights with one lance. Philip fled panic-stricken over the river Epte on an aged horse called Morel, which he had chosen because it was easy to ride, but the bridge gave way and he, Morel and his knights were thrown into the water. Twenty of them were drowned and Philip himself escaped with difficulty.

Richard boasted in a letter to the bishop of Durham how 'the king of the French drank river water on that day'. One hundred French knights were captured—Philip's heaviest loss so far—and the English king reconquered the entire Vexin.

From her retirement at Fontevrault Eleanor made one of her rare interventions in these days. Philip of Dreux, the bishop of Beauvais, was still immured in a dungeon at Château-Gaillard. The papal legate, cardinal Peter of Capua, asked Richard to release him, arguing that it was contrary to Christian law to imprison a bishop. The king answered the cardinal with furious abuse, shouting that the pope had never done anything to help him when he was a prisoner, that the bishop was no better than a brigand, and that the cardinal was himself a traitor, a liar, a simoniac and a suborner. He ended by telling Peter to get out and never cross his path again. But the queen mother had obviously taken the measure of the new pope, Innocent III, who was to prove the most formidable pontiff of the Middle Ages. She arranged for the bishop of Beauvais to escape, even offering him a refuge. She was much too clever to let her son add pope Innocent to his enemies, and was quite prepared to brave the royal anger.

Eleanor's interference appears all the more shrewd in the light of Philip II's marital situation. A widower, he decided to remarry and his choice was the king of Denmark's sister, the fifteen-year-old princess Ingeborg. However, although she was a girl of great beauty, during the marriage service Philip was suddenly seized by a physical aversion to her that he found impossible to overcome. Almost at once he began to look openly for a fresh consort. Poor Ingeborg remained in France and appealed to Rome, which promptly excommunicated the king of the French. Nevertheless, in 1199 Philip defiantly married a Tyrolese lady, Agnes of Meran, who presented him with several children while Ingeborg continued to languish in a convent at Soissons. Innocent III was hardly the person to tolerate such flagrant sinfulness in an anointed king.

Philip already had enough trouble with secular matters. In 1197 the emperor Henry VI had died before his time, although he had managed to conquer Sicily. Henry's heir was his son, the infant king of Sicily who—as the emperor Frederick II and the 'Wonder of the World', *Stupor mundi*—would one day astonish and alarm all Christendom. But Frederick was still a baby and the German princes had grown weary of the terrible house of Hohenstaufen. In 1198 Richard personally attended the imperial election of Cologne and made sure that the new emperor was his nephew, Otto of Brunswick; all those friendships with German magnates during the final months of the king's captivity were turned to good account. Yet another of Eleanor's grandchildren had found a crown, although he had to relinquish Aquitaine and could no longer inherit the Angevin empire. Furthermore, Otto IV was married to the daughter of the duke of Lorraine and therefore constituted a potential threat to king Philip's northern borders.

By 1199, despite Philip II's undoubted ability, the Capetian monarchy's hopes of expansion were beginning to appear very bleak. England and the Angevin empire were under the iron grip of Richard, who was a far abler soldier than his father had ever been; Château-Gaillard was as much a symbol of aggression as of defence. Although the English king's vassals were as turbulent and rebellious as always, they had an increasing respect for his military talent, and the great feudatories of France were becoming more ready to join the Plantagenet against a liege lord who had been outlawed by the Church. Although Richard was in his forty-second year (advanced middle age for a mediaeval man), he was none the less plainly in the best of health, having thrown off all those ailments that had afflicted him at the beginning of his reign and during the crusade. It must have seemed that at any moment he would inflict some disastrous reverse on the French king.

The Death of Richard

Early in 1199 a Limousin peasant ploughing his field at Châlus, not far from Limoges, turned up a rich Gallo-Roman treasure horde. It included a marvellous gold model of a king or emperor seated at a table with his family. The peasant took it to his lord, Achard of Châlus, from whom it was claimed by his overlord, the viscount of Limoges. Rumours about so fabulous a treasure soon spread all over France. Aymar of Limoges was Richard's vassal, and the king, as was his right in feudal law, duly demanded that it be handed over to him at once. The viscount offered to surrender half of it, but no more. Meanwhile the wonderful treasure stayed at Châlus.

Richard needed money desperately. His mercenaries were mutinous from lack of pay, and in consequence were as much a scourge of the Angevin lands as of those of king Philip. Normandy, once so loyal, had been driven to the brink of rebellion by excessive taxation. Indeed at about this time the king wrote a frivolous song, addressed to the dauphin of Auvergne, about his penury:

> *Savies qu'a Chinon non a argent ni denier*
> (There's neither silver nor one penny at Chinon)

Understandably Richard was determined to obtain such a valuable treasure as that found at Châlus, and the viscount's proposed compromise infuriated him, hardening his resolve. He marched on Châlus, regardless of the fact that it was Lent—traditionally a season of peace—and laid siege to the castle.

Châlus was garrisoned by only fifty men, mainly peasants led by a handful of knights. Foolishly they decided to resist the king, sending word to the viscount of Limoges to come and relieve them. Richard anticipated scant difficulty in reducing this rustic stronghold and his skilled engineers began to undermine its walls, with considerable effect. During the late evening of 25 March, after they had had supper, the king and Mercadier went on horseback to see how the work was progressing. Archers shot

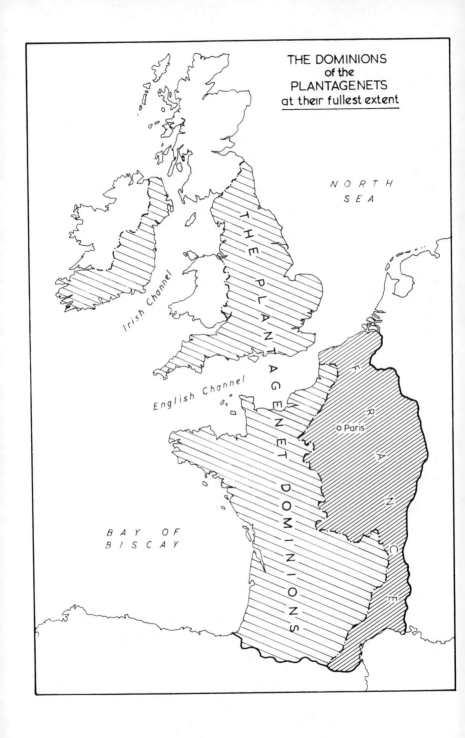

THE DOMINIONS
of the
PLANTAGENETS
at their fullest extent

NORTH
SEA

THE PLANTAGENET DOMINIONS

Irish Channel

English Channel

BAY OF
BISCAY

o Paris

FRANCE

at them from the ramparts, but Richard relied on his shield to protect him. Suddenly a bolt from a crossbow hit him in the shoulder, just below the neck. He rode calmly back to his lodgings, for he was no stranger to wounds. When the surgeons pulled the bolt out, however, the shaft broke; the head seems to have become hooked onto the king's spine. Eventually, after an agonizing operation, they succeeded in digging it out, but a piece of iron remained. Gangrene set in. Richard realized that he was going to die and sent for his mother.

Eleanor, who had been keeping Lent at Fontevrault, came at once, accompanied by the abbot of Turpenay. She also sent abbess Matilda of Fontevrault to fetch count John and to inform queen Berengaria. The king prepared for death in an edifying manner, making a public confession in which he repented of betraying his father, of making war in Lent and of refusing to take communion because of his hatred for Philip II. He also announced that he was prepared to wait in purgatory until the Last Judgment to atone for his sins. He then received holy communion, which he had not done since he was on crusade. When the castle fell, the young crossbowman who had shot the fatal bolt was brought before him. 'You killed my father and my brother', said the boy defiantly, 'and you can do what you want to me. I am not sorry.' But Richard pardoned him, saying, 'Leave in peace. I forgive you for my death and will take no revenge. Enjoy the daylight, as my gift.' The queen mother arrived 'as though borne by the wind', and Richard died in her arms on the evening of 6 April 1199—'as the day ended, so ended his life'. The king had asked for his heart to be interred at his 'faithful city' of Rouen, near his brother Henry; his body itself was buried at Fontevrault at the foot of his father, as a sign of repentance for having rebelled against him.

Richard I was the magnificent one of Eleanor's offspring. She had called him 'the great one' without exaggeration. Troubadours and chroniclers paid him many tributes. Gaucelm Faidit, one of the king's protégés, laments in a *planh* that 'never again will there be a man so generous, so courtly, so hardy, so bountiful' as *Richartz, reys dels Engles*, and compares him to Arthur and Charlemagne and even to Alexander the Great. Although Richard had been cruel, perverse and extravagant, he had also been a mighty warrior and a figure of genuine splendour. He has had much criticism from modern English historians from Stubbs onwards, because they were offended by his lack of interest in England and the English, whom he regarded as little more than a source of money and troops. All the same, contemporary Englishmen were devoted to him, and when he was actually in their country his government was firm and efficient. In Palestine and France he was indisputably a success as a soldier and as a statesman.

It was Richard's fortune and misfortune to be Eleanor's son. Although not so intelligent as his mother, in more than a few ways he was a male Eleanor. Both were true Latins, people of the south, who had nothing in common with the northern French (in these days Poitevins were hardly thought of as northerners), let alone the English. Both were realists and both were masterful, greedy for power, ruthless yet subtle politicians and diplomatists, although, to a certain extent, Richard lacked his mother's self-control and delicate touch. He also was a patron of troubadours and a troubadour himself, which must have delighted Eleanor's heart. He was like her too in showing both magnanimity and harshness in personal relationships, and in being frivolous and ironical, with a cynical, sarcastic streak, but at the same time a devout Christian. Above all, although there is of course no proper evidence, one must suspect that Richard's feelings for his mother were excessive, and that he had to pay for them. His respect and admiration for her precluded interest in any other women. This is surely in part at least the explanation for his homosexuality and for his exaggerated and peculiarly personal cult of chivalry.

For Eleanor the shock of Richard's death must have been the most terrible event in her life, the loss of 'the staff of my age, the light of my eyes'. It has been pointed out that whereas in documents referring to John she uses the normal *dilectus* (beloved), in those that refer to Richard she employs the word *carissimus* (most dear), and this was obviously not by accident. She personally superintended his interment at Fontevrault, with St Hugh of Lincoln to sing the requiem. To ensure the nuns' prayers she gave a magnificent bequest that provided an annual sum to pay for every nun's habit. In addition she made a multitude of donations to other abbeys to pray for his soul, and gave many rich gifts to members of his household; several years later she is found giving a present to a certain Roger who had been one of the king's cooks. Even so, despite her bereavement, the queen mother was not a woman to waste time mourning. Her need to rule was nearly as great as her love for her favourite son.

17 King John

'Your strong possession, much more than your right;
Or else it must go wrong with you, and me:
So much my conscience whispers in your ear;
Which none but heaven, and you, and I, shall hear.'
Shakespeare, *King John*

'Et ne connais-tu pas l'implacable Agrippine?'
Racine, *Britannicus*

The new king of England and lord of all the Angevin empire was to be count John. There was of course a rival claimant, twelve-year-old Arthur, duke of Brittany, who had in some ways a better claim in feudal law. He was the son of the third of Henry II's sons who had lived to manhood, whereas John was only the fourth son, and at one time Richard had treated duke Arthur as his heir. On his deathbed, however, Richard apparently designated John as his heir—at least, according to John's close friend and supporter, William of Braose (who was present), and to Eleanor.

Although there is no proof, one may guess that Eleanor was largely responsible for the alteration in the succession. It is even possible that she connived at misrepresenting Richard's last words. Admittedly there were many arguments against Arthur. His mother Constance, the heiress of the previous Breton dynasty, was no lover of Plantagents even if she was the mother of one; she had intrigued with Philip of France against Richard, and in 1196 her troops had fought against the English king. Naturally all this might change if Arthur succeeded his uncle. On the other hand John, supported by his mother, would have the best chance of keeping the Angevin empire intact. Constance was little known outside Brittany and Maine, and only Eleanor could hold Poitou and Aquitaine. Furthermore, the feudal law of inheritance varied in the different Angevin territories: in some areas John had a better legal claim as the late king's younger brother.

The near-contemporary biographer of William Marshal recounts a revealing conversation between his hero and the archbishop of Canterbury and justiciar, Hubert Walter, about the succession. The archbishop was at first for Arthur, but William argued that the young duke 'has bad advisers and is arrogant and violent. If we have him for our master we shall be sorry, as he dislikes the English.' The great soldier persuaded the archbishop that the only possible choice was John. Nonetheless Hubert told

219

William, 'You will regret this more than any decision of your entire life'. Arthur was only a boy, and it looks as though William Marshal distrusted not Arthur but Constance. It may also be relevant that William had been close to the queen mother ever since she had been his patron when he was a young man.

Eleanor's preference of John to Arthur must surely reflect her enduring need for power. Probably she had little affection for John, let alone confidence in his abilities. But had Arthur succeeded she would almost certainly have been displaced by Constance and have lost every vestige of influence; worse, she might have been deprived of both Poitou and Aquitaine, which she had recovered with so much difficulty. And Eleanor was not the sort of woman to live peaceably with a daughter-in-law, other than some faceless nonentity such as poor Berengaria.

John was now thirty-one years old. Unlike his golden brother, he was an ugly little man, only 5 feet 5 inches tall, who with age grew fat and bald. Nor was he a Spartan campaigner like Richard, though devoted to hunting and hawking and constantly in the saddle; in contrast, he disliked warfare and even tournaments, and was a coward at heart. This new king loved luxury, and had the reputation of being a glutton and a drunkard, who never kept the prescribed days of fasting and abstinence. He was a lecher, known to have fathered at last seven bastards. He was much the best-read member of his family—Eleanor excepted—with a questioning interest in theology that was sharpened by his innate scepticism. Although fond of music, however, he had not inherited his dynasty's love of poetry and troubadours, but he possessed to the full its peculiar brand of sardonic humour. The Easter that he ascended the throne, bishop Hugh of Lincoln rebuked him publicly for not receiving holy communion (something he had not done since he was a boy) and showed him a carving of the Last Judgment, pointing to a scene of damned souls being dragged down to hell by demons; John calmly pulled the saint to the other side, which represented the souls of the saved ascending to heaven, and said, 'Let's look at these instead—I am going to go with them'. He delighted in shocking clerics with his frivolous and often blasphemous wit. Nevertheless, he knew how to please, possessing a honeyed charm like that of his brothers, and could even inspire loyalty.

In recent years there has been a misguided tendency to whitewash king John. His evil reputation is dismissed as a plot concocted by the clerical chroniclers because of his quarrel with the Church, or else as the result of applying 'Victorian standards'. Admittedly some contemporary writers (in particular, Roger of Wendover) are clearly unreliable, and give a distorted picture. But the picture of a thoroughly wicked man carries conviction. It is claimed that modern mediaevalists who know the sources have arrived at a fairer picture of the king. Yet the same sources were examined by experts in the 1940s and 1950s—not to mention bishop Stubbs and Sir Maurice Powicke—who all accept the traditional portrait. In fact there is every reason to believe that the king was very bad indeed—'nature's enemy', as Matthew Paris calls him.

Beyond question John had many gifts. At times he could be an extremely shrewd politician, a most able diplomatist, an energetic administrator and—on a single occasion—a truly brilliant general. Yet his good qualities were outweighed by his bad ones. In the words of his most convincing modern biographer, Dr Warren, John 'had the mental abilities of a great king, but the inclinations of a petty tyrant'. For John's character was flawed through and through, 'light, profligate and perfidious'. He was fundamentally frivolous, and prone to fits of almost pathological idleness. He lacked both honour and honesty, and was also horribly cruel and cowardly. Indeed he was all but a caricature of a bad king: some historians have even found something comic in his exaggerated wickedness, an element of *Grand Guignol*. But contemporaries saw nothing amusing in this wolfish man. Few rulers have aroused such hatred among all classes of their subjects, let alone in their opponents.

As has been seen, Eleanor's original choice as Richard's successor was Otto of Brunswick, who had disqualified himself by becoming emperor. However, the queen mother must have known that she was the one person who could control John. Even if he could never fill the place of Richard, he would at least guarantee her power and independence in Poitou and Aquitaine. One may guess that, for his part, John both trusted and feared her. Moreover, not only did his mother know how to make use of his undoubted qualities and how to guard against his terrible weaknesses, but in herself she was a most valuable ally who could still act as his lieutenant if necessary. Had she been a little younger, he might have had a less disastrous reign.

Undoubtedly Eleanor played a considerable part in ensuring that it was John, and not Arthur, who succeeded Richard. William Marshal and archbishop Hubert Walter and also his half-brother, archbishop Geoffrey Plantagenet of York—made certain of England for him, but they must have been greatly helped by the public knowledge that John was the queen mother's choice. For by now Eleanor was a popular, even revered, figure with the English: from the time of her release from captivity in 1189 the chroniclers write of her with growing respect. Richard of Devizes eulogizes her: 'Queen Eleanor, a woman beyond compare, beautiful and chaste, powerful but modest and meek yet eloquent, which is something rarely met with in a woman.' It may well be that her intervention in John's favour decided William Marshal and the archbishop, together with many other magnates who might otherwise have rejected him. As it was, if Constance's men had captured John—which very nearly happened—Arthur would have become king.

John rushed to Chinon to take possession of his brother's treasure, without realizing how quickly his sister-in-law would move. Within twelve days of Richard's death, Constance (who had just married a Poitevin noble, Guy of Thouars) rode into Angers at the head of a Breton army, and the lords of Anjou, Maine and Touraine declared for Arthur; a skilled soldier, William of Les Roches, was then appointed as the young duke's seneschal of Anjou. John escaped in the nick of time, fleeing to Normandy, whence he crossed to England. Shakespeare makes Queen Elinor say to John, not implausibly,

> What now, my son? Have I not ever said,
> How that ambitious Constance would not cease,
> Till she had kindled France, and all the world,
> Upon the right and party of her son?

King Philip speedily took advantage of this promising situation, invading Normandy and capturing Evreux. Fortunately for John, William Marshal had made sure of the Normans' loyalty before his departure for England. The garrisons held out, halting the enemy's advance. John could feel that Normandy was safe enough while he was being crowned king of the English.

In the meantime Eleanor captured the rest of the Angevin empire for her son. As Sir Maurice Powicke emphasizes, 'The contest in western France resolved itself into a duel between Constance and the old queen. . . . Eleanor, as duchess, made a grand tour through Poitou and the Bordelais. All interests of barons, clergy and towns were secured'. She had already enlisted the help of Mercadier and his ferocious Brabançon mercenaries, who were laying all Anjou waste in John's name. Constance and Arthur were forced to retreat from Angers into Maine, taking refuge in the capital, Le Mans. John returned from England and his troops advanced on Le Mans, which they quickly stormed and put to the sword; those townsmen who survived the massacre were carried off as prisoners by the Brabançons, and the walls of Le Mans were razed to the ground. Constance and Arthur had escaped by night, finding a temporary haven at Tours. Here Constance handed her child to king Philip, who sent him to Paris to be brought up with his own son. He was only too pleased to accept Arthur's homage as count of Anjou and Maine. But the entire Angevin empire was now in John's possession.

Eleanor's grand tour, which had contributed so much to this outcome, had been a most strenuous business for such an old woman. The stately but urgent progress began in April and ended in July. It took her to all her more important towns, including London, Poitiers, Niort, La Rochelle, Saintes, Bordeaux and many others. To five of these towns she gave charters that freed their inhabitants of any feudal obligations and allowed them to set up corporations. Her purpose was to see that her vassals remained loyal to her and with her son she used every gift and stratagem in her power. She bought the friendship of any lord who might waver; thus Raoul of Mauléon, who had inconvenient claims on La Rochelle, was compensated with the ducal hunting lodge of Talmont, which had once been a favourite residence of her father and grandfather. Although it owed much to good road and river communications, the speed and extent of her progress was an astonishing achievement. Her administrative activity is still more impressive, the most energetic period in her life to judge from the surviving documents.

In July 1199 Eleanor performed what must have been the most difficult and distasteful task of all. She went to Tours, knelt at the feet of her sons' bitterest enemy, king Philip, and personally paid homage for her lands. By doing so she had—in strict feudal law, at least—effectively blocked Arthur's claims to Poitou and Aquitaine. This done, she drew up a deed resigning them to her son, but retaining the usufruct for her lifetime.

She then journeyed to Normandy, where at Rouen on 30 July 1199 she met John, who had been consecrated as duke of the Normans and crowned as king of the English since she had last seen him, largely thanks to her. For once he showed sound sense and was careful not to antagonize his mother. He knew her need for power and made no attempt to obtain complete control of

Poitou and Aquitaine, issuing an edict to the effect that she was to keep them all her life and stating that, 'We desire that she shall be lady not only of all those territories which are ours, but also of ourself and of all our lands and possessions'. In practice a sort of condominium between Eleanor and John came into existence in Poitou, and probably in Aquitaine as well; there is no doubt that the king recognized Eleanor as being in some sense a sovereign prince who was his equal in these lands, even though she allowed him to appoint the seneschals. (The latter included Robert of Thornham, a knight from Kent and a former crusading comrade of Richard's, who for a time held both seneschalships.) Furthermore, John also made a point of continuing to pay her 'queen's gold', although legally this was the perquisite of the queen consort and not of the queen mother. But the king had good cause to be grateful.

It is worth pointing out here that John was not exactly noted for gratitude and was not always so considerate where his female relatives were concerned. Indeed he was scarcely a man to set much store by family ties. He swiftly cheated the unfortunate Berengaria out of the county of Maine, which had been her marriage settlement. In 1201 the king made a graceful gesture by way of compensation, promising his sister-in-law an entire town in Normandy together with two castles in Anjou and a large annual income, but in the event she received nothing. Three years later the pope wrote indignantly to John that queen Berengaria was so poor that she was having to 'live like a beggar' at the expense of her sister, the countess of Champagne. Yet despite further angry letters from Innocent III she was unable to obtain any redress until 1215, and even then she was kept in arrears. Eventually Berengaria was wise enough to put her affairs in the hands of those accomplished businessmen the Templars, who managed to extract sufficient money from the English crown to allow her to lead a comfortable and pious life near Le Mans till she died in 1230.

By September 1199 duke Arthur's supporters were falling out with Philip. The French king had occupied far too many of the castles in Maine and Anjou that had stayed loyal to Arthur, installing French garrisons and presumptuously demolishing the stronghold of Balun; men began to suspect that the king's occupation might be permanent. Arthur's two chief supporters—Amaury, viscount of Thouars (Constance's brother-in-law) and William of Les Roches—entered into secret communication with John. They, Constance and the young duke then left Paris without Philip's knowledge and went to John, whom they met near the ruins of Le Mans. A brief acquaintance with the new king of the English was quite sufficient to disillusion them, however, and they fled for a second time. The exception was William of Les Roches, who realized which way the wind was blowing and went over to John. He was rewarded by being made hereditary seneschal of Anjou, Maine and Touraine. But though an excellent soldier, he was a dangerous subject, proud and independent. It is likely that the queen mother met him often, as William's new headquarters were at Chinon, near Fontevrault, and he witnessed at least one of her charters.

No doubt the loyalty of the English made John's cause appear even more impressively solid. This loyalty was in large part due to his surprising good sense in appointing Hubert Walter as his chancellor. After Richard I's return Hubert had shown his remarkable gifts as an administrator, being as imaginative as he was efficient. He quickly paid off the arrears of Richard's ransom by introducing—for the first time in English history—a wealth tax, imposing a swingeing levy on lands and on goods and chattels, and by some miracle he managed to do so without provoking a rebellion. Unlike William Longchamp, Hubert never inspired personal dislike. He was masterful without being arrogant and always ruled in the king's name, never in his own. He was also splendidly hospitable. But he could not hope to avoid arousing opposition in the long term, and from 1196 onwards

Richard's steadily increasing demands for money made his position more and more difficult. In the end, most unwillingly, Richard had dismissed him at the prompting of pope Innocent, who did not think it seemly that an archbishop should serve as a secular chancellor. As has been seen, Hubert—after being persuaded by William Marshal—had played a crucial role in securing the throne for John. Moreover at the coronation in Westminster abbey on Ascension day he not only crowned the king, but read out an eloquently phrased defence of elective monarchy. He was truly a most formidable minister and when John heard of the archbishop's death in 1205, he exclaimed 'Now I am king of England for the first time!' While he lived, Hubert was to some extent a guarantee of good government and his chancellorship gave John an undeserved aura of respectability. No doubt it reassured even the queen mother.

Not altogether unexpectedly, William Marshal also continued to support king John. William, as the greatest soldier of his age, was widely admired and respected. In his mid-fifties, despite the wear and tear of countless campaigns and tournaments he remained as vigorous and enterprising as ever. In person he was a big, handsome, brown-haired man with a majestic carriage that a contemporary biographer compared to that of a Roman emperor. His code of honour was as punctilious and genuine as it was Arthurian and he proved as unshakeably loyal to the new king as he had been to Henry II and Richard I. (William is an excellent testimony to the good judgment of Eleanor, who, it will be remembered, had recognized his sterling qualities many years before.) Although John had little in common with a man of such nobility, he was shrewd enough to appoint William as earl marshal, in which capacity he became more or less the king's chief of staff in military matters.

John's triumph seemed assured by the end of 1199. For the time being, Arthur and his followers did not renew their alliance with Philip II, who was himself in serious difficulties. His dispute with pope Innocent had come to a head, and on 13 January 1200 France was put under a papal interdict that deprived it of all religious ministry: no priest was allowed to give holy communion to any of Philip's subjects, nor to marry or bury them. Moreover the emperor Otto IV was as much the ally of king John as he had been of king Richard. Although far from beaten, Philip realized that this was not the moment to fight for the Angevin empire. On 22 May 1200 he and John met at the castle of Le Goulet on the Seine, where they swiftly agreed on a treaty. The French king acknowledged John as rightful count of Anjou and Maine, besides recognizing him as overlord of Brittany; in return John surrendered the Vexin and the county of Evreux, and abandoned his by now totally unrealistic claims to Berry and the Auvergne. In addition the English king promised to pay a 'relief' of 20,000 marks to provide a dowry for a Castilian princess, one of John's nieces, who was to marry Philip's son and heir, the future Louis VIII.

The treaty was a triumph for Eleanor. It meant that she had totally outwitted Constance. Some Englishmen grumbled that Richard I would never have given away so much, although in calling John 'soft sword' they were tacitly admitting that he could hardly hope to be as formidable a soldier as his brother. Indeed, John had done well enough, being recognized by the French king as the lawful heir to almost all Richard's lands on both sides of the Channel. News arrived that the duchess Constance had contracted the severe leprosy of which she was to die in the following year. It seemed as though the Angevin empire was going to survive after all, under the ruler of Eleanor's choice. The projected marriage—which she may well have planned—between Philip's son and Eleanor's grand-daughter was to be the guarantee of its secure future.

18 The Grandmother of Europe

'If the queen of England thinks a person good enough for her daughter, what have other people got to say?'

Queen Victoria

'her [Eleanor's] better points come out most strongly in her old age, when we see her, between seventy and eighty years old, running about from one end of Europe to another to patch up truces and to make peaces. . . . She had engaged in a lifelong quarrel with her first husband in 1150, and with her second in 1173; now in 1200 she fetches a grand-daughter of the second to marry the grandson of the first, as a pledge of harmony between the sons of the two.'

Bishop Stubbs

18 The Grandmother of Europe

'If the queen of England thinks a person good enough for her daughter, what have other people got to say?'

Queen Victoria

'her [Eleanor's] better points come out most strongly in her old age, when we see her, between seventy and eighty years old, running about from one end of Europe to another to patch up truces and to make peaces. . . . She had engaged in a lifelong quarrel with her first husband in 1150, and with her second in 1173; now in 1200 she fetches a grand-daughter of the second to marry the grandson of the first, as a pledge of harmony between the sons of the two.'

Bishop Stubbs

One may claim without exaggeration that as a dynast Eleanor of Aquitaine was very much a precursor of queen Victoria. The soubriquet 'grandmother of Europe' has been bestowed on the latter, but it belongs no less to Eleanor. Her daughters were the queens of Castile and Sicily, and the consorts of the counts of Blois, Champagne and Toulouse and the duke of Saxony. Two grandsons were Holy Roman Emperors and another three were kings of England, Castile and Jerusalem. Her grand-daughters sat on the thrones of France, Portugal and Scotland, and an illegitimate one was princess of Wales. Louis IX, '*Saint Louis*', who was to be the most venerated of all French kings, was one of her great–grandsons. Furthermore, her son John's descendants in the direct male line were to rule England until 1485.

She had always taken care to arrange good marriages for her daughters. Apart from that of Joanna to Raymond of Toulouse, they appear to have been successful enough from a worldly viewpoint. Indeed, when making such alliances the old queen may even have taken personal considerations into account, remembering her own unhappy marriages. In 1199 she must surely have been deeply affected not only by Richard's death but also by the tragic end of Joanna of Toulouse. By now, of all Eleanor's daughters only Eleanor of Castile was still alive, and no doubt her mother wished to see her again. But surely the old woman's principal reason for visiting Spain, and for undertaking so wearisome a journey at her great age, was to choose the more suitable of her two unmarried Castilian grand-daughters as a bride for king Philip's son. As has already been said, she probably believed that the future of the Angevin empire could depend on this marriage.

Accordingly the queen mother set out for Castile in December 1199, even before her son had made peace with king Philip. Perhaps ironically she found herself threatened by an ambush, as on so many of her journeys in the past. This time it was successful, although she had a formidable escort that included not only the

ELEANOR'S FAMILY BY HENRY II

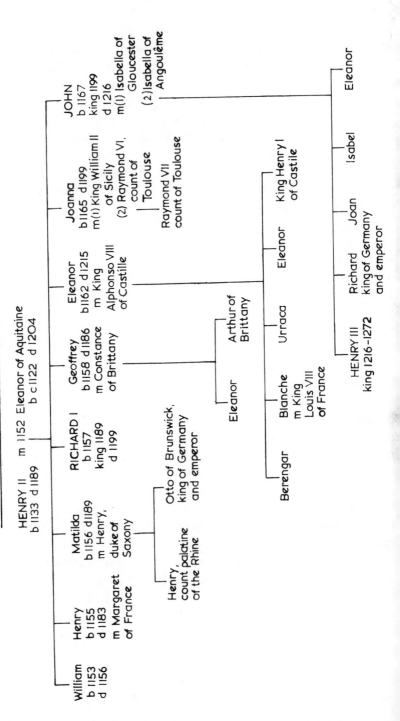

archbishop of Bordeaux but also the redoubtable Mercadier, who had entered her service. The no doubt indignant old queen found herself the captive of her long-standing enemies, the Lusignan family, having been taken prisoner by Hugh IX of Lusignan, 'Hugh the Brown'; he demanded that she should reinstate him in his father's county of La Marche, of which he was overlord. Eleanor had no option but to agree; the alternative was a humiliating and frustrating captivity.

The queen mother reached Castile in the middle of January 1200, so she must have crossed the Pyrenees in the depths of winter, presumably through the pass of Roncesvalles, riding over the snow. We do not know exactly where she joined the Castilian court, but it was probably at the capital, Toledo, or at Burgos. In its own way this was a court as opulent and exotic as those of Jerusalem and Sicily, filled with Moorish luxuries and slaves. Moreover, like those at Poitiers in the old days, its courtiers knew how to appreciate Provençal verse and the songs of the troubadours, many of whom had found a sympathetic refuge in Castile. King Alfonso VIII—'the Noble'—was a brilliant figure, as cultivated as he was warlike and a patron of literature. His marriage to Eleanor's daughter seems to have been a happy one and they had eleven children.

There was an abundance of marriageable royal daughters in Castile. One was already betrothed to the future king of Leon, but there were two others. The elder, Urraca, seems to have been considered the obvious choice and no doubt expected to be chosen on grounds of seniority. Yet Eleanor was not easy to please, as both Alice of France and Constance of Brittany had discovered. The dictatorial old lady decided that she preferred the youngest of her Castilian grand-daughters, Blanca, who was just thirteen. Eleanor's somewhat unconvincing reason was that the name Urraca would seem too harsh and unmusical to French ears, whereas that of Blanca would sound better across the Pyrenees. Urraca would have to be content with the kingdom of

Portugal. The old queen's choice was to be justified. Blanca's son, St Louis, would owe much to his Castilian mother. Shakespeare preserves the memory of her beauty:

> If lusty love should go in quest of beauty,
> Where should he find it fairer than in Blanch?
> If zealous love should go in search of virtue,
> Where should he find it purer than in Blanch?
> If love ambitious sought a match of birth,
> Whose veins bound richer blood than lady Blanch?

Eleanor remained in Spain for two months. Her long stay may have been partly due to exhaustion, but in any case no marriage could be solemnized during Lent, so there was no urgency. Nevertheless she and her grand-daughter left in good time to be able to celebrate Easter at Bordeaux, which they reached during Holy Week. Here the old queen—and indeed king John—suffered a serious loss: on Easter Monday, Mercadier was killed by another mercenary in a duel. Eleanor had been deprived of her best general. Grandmother and grand-daughter continued the journey without further incident and in May Blanca—henceforward known as Blanche—was married to Louis of France by the archbishop of Bordeaux. The service had to take place in Normandy, because France was still under pope Innocent's interdict. But Eleanor was not present. She had gone back to Fontevrault, nowadays her only real home, 'worn out by the labours of her journey and by old age'. No doubt she confidently expected the marriage to establish a lasting peace between Capetian and Plantagenet. She had reckoned without king John's own match-making.

The English king had been married to Isabella of Gloucester since he was twenty-one (indeed, he had been betrothed to her since he was nine) and he must once have been profoundly grateful to gain the hand of the heiress to the richest earldom in England. But unfortunately Isabella was childless and, to judge from the number and age of his bastards, the king had frequently consoled himself with mistresses for several years. The contemporary chronicler of the dukes of Normandy (on the whole a trustworthy witness) refers to John's notorious lechery, calling him 'cruel towards all men and too covetous of pretty ladies'. He also seems to have liked young girls, a weakness that was to involve him in serious trouble.

In 1199 John divorced Isabella of Gloucester, although she had only recently been crowned with him. It was all too easy to obtain an annulment from Innocent III on the grounds of consanguinity, as she was his second cousin and shared Henry I of England with him as a great-grandfather. The king had no desire to be succeeded by Arthur, who was the only other surviving Plantagenet. He therefore sent envoys to king Sancho of Portugal to ask for the hand of his daughter. But suddenly, at the very last moment, he changed his mind and forgot the Portugese alliance altogether.

While the English envoys were in Portugal during the summer of 1200, king John was making a progress through Poitou. The dangerous Lusignan family had now become his allies since they had got possession of La Marche, and to make the reconciliation complete John visited them at Lusignan, where he was splendidly received. Amid all the festivities he was presented to the beautiful Isabella of Angoulême, the daughter and heiress of count Aymar of Angoulême. She was no more than fourteen—perhaps only twelve—and was betrothed to the head of the Lusignan clan, count Hugh the Brown (the man who had recently ambushed queen Eleanor on her way to Castile), and in 1200 a formal betrothal was almost as binding as a marriage that had been comsummated. Although he himself was thirty-five John immediately fell in love with the girl, and where his lusts were concerned the king had no restraint whatsoever. (William of Newburgh tells us that John hated a certain Eustace fitz John simply because he had placed 'a common woman' in the royal bed instead of his own wife.) Moreover, it was rumoured that the young Isabella actually enticed the king and led him on. Hugh the Brown, unsuspecting and only too anxious to be of service to his generous overlord, was sent on a mission to England to keep him out of the way. To Hugh's complete surprise, he suddenly received news in August that king John had just married his betrothed at Angoulême with her father's full approval.

As a marriage the alliance was reasonably successful. Isabella of Angoulême gave the king all the children he wanted, although he still kept plenty of mistresses. She herself, it was rumoured, was promiscuous and John was even said to have imprisoned her on occasions. But this seems to be a smear put about by the king's enemies and is not supported by any convincing evidence.

Diplomatically the marriage was a disaster. Some historians argue unconvincingly that John's marriage to Isabella of Angoulême was a carefully considered move. It is true that she was the heiress of the count of Angoulême, who was also the half-brother of the count of Limoges and had a better claim to La Marche than Hugh the Brown. But the king must have known that he was exchanging one new friend for a host of enemies. And it is perfectly clear that by accepting Hugh's occupation of La Marche John had hoped to secure his loyalty. Hugh would never forgive the loss of his prospects of succeeding to the county of Angoulême. Moreover, he may well have loved Isabella for her own sake: after the king's death he eventually managed to marry her. John's passion for his child bride was so great that men said that he seemed as if chained to his bed. On the whole, then, the traditional story that John was overcome by lust, and disregarded every other consideration, carries conviction.

The Lusignan family were numerous and energetic. Besides Hugh there was his brother Ralph, count of Eu, their uncle Geoffrey, and his two sons. All were excellent soldiers; they were also rich and powerful, and allied to barons throughout Poitou and, to a lesser extent, Normandy. They were determined to have their revenge, and early in 1201 they rose in revolt. Eleanor, who was ill after her journey, knew that if the Lusignan rising was mishandled, serious trouble would ensue. In February she wrote from Fontevrault to John in England about the situation. Her letter is curiously intimate, almost chatty. 'I wish to tell you, my very dear son, that during my sickness I invited our cousin Amaury of Thouars to come and see me, and the pleasure of his visit did me a great deal of good. Only he, out of all your barons in Poitou has not done us any injury or stolen any of your lands. . . . He has promised to do everything he can to recover for you these lands and castles.' It was something of an achievement to win over viscount Amaury, who was Arthur's uncle by marriage and a former enemy. But most of the Poitevin lords supported the Lusignan faction or at least sympathized with them. In addition, their friends in Normandy began to stir, although John largely forestalled trouble here by ordering his seneschal to seize all Lusignan castles.

It was only a matter of time before king Philip would try to exploit the quarrel. By his lust and stupidity John had doomed the peace by which his mother set such store. Her brave journey to Castile had not, after all, saved the Angevin empire.

19 The Murder of Arthur

'The death
Of young wolves is never to be pitied.'
The Duchess of Malfi

'So the king's counsellors . . . suggested that he
should order the noble youth to be deprived of
his eyes and genitals.'

Ralph of Coggeshall

When king John landed in Normandy in May 1201 he did not suspect that he was on the verge of a great war, nor had he any reason to do so. Admittedly the Lusignan family were still in revolt, but he had taken practical steps to cow them; their castles in Poitou and Normandy had been captured or were besieged, and his troops would soon be harrying their lands in La Marche. And as yet the rebels had not appealed to Philip of France, who was showing no sign of wishing to intervene. Indeed, after entertaining the French king on the Norman border, John and Isabella of Angoulême visited him in Paris, where he lent them his palace. During the visit Philip retired to Fontainebleau with queen Agnes, who was seriously ill and about to die. Both monarchs appear to have reached full agreement over their policies—though no details are known of their discussions—and John and Isabella gave themselves up to enjoyment in the French capital.

However, the Lusignan revolt refused to die down. John would not demean himself by diplomacy, although the rebels might easily have been bought off, and accused them of treason. Most unfairly, instead of offering them a proper hearing in his ducal court, he ordered them to prove their innocence in a trial by combat in which he himself would be represented by professional champions. After this his opponents took the obvious step of appealing to Philip, who was his overlord. Meanwhile John continued to attack them and lay waste their lands, seizing Raoul of Lusignan's castle of Drincourt and confiscating his county of Eu. Then, in April 1202, the French king summoned John as his vassal to come to Paris and appear before his high court and answer the Lusignan charges.

As might have been expected, John refused to appear and denied Philip's right to hear the case. Accordingly, on 28 April the latter declared war and struck almost immediately down the Seine into north-east Normandy, capturing Aumâle, Boutevant, Gournai and other Norman castles of vital strategic importance, and besieging Arques, the fortress that protected Dieppe. Philip had clearly prepared his campaign in some detail, and with his dogged determination was once again planning to destroy the entire Angevin empire, or at least to dismember it.

At the end of April the king of France formally betrothed his baby daughter to Arthur. Two months later he publicly received the young duke's homage for Brittany, Anjou, Maine and Touraine, and also for Poitou. In strict feudal law Philip had no right whatsoever to give Poitou to duke Arthur, as he had received his grandmother's homage, which was still valid. It was the plainest possible way of announcing that he meant to overthrow completely the Angevin dominion in France. Furthermore, the treaty that Philip and Arthur now concluded specifically denied the latter any right to Normandy. 'Concerning Normandy', the treaty stipulated, 'the king of the French shall keep what he has already gained and also what it may please God to let him gain in the future'. Arthur was then publicly knighted by Philip, and sent off to conquer Poitou.

In the meantime king John was making his own preparations for a counter-attack and had assembled an army in southern Normandy. Knowing that he would have to fight on two fronts, however, he moved his headquarters to Le Mans, from where he would be able to supervise operations in both Normandy and Poitou while keeping well away from the actual fighting. Here on 30 July 1202 he received alarming news.

Eleanor had been warned, just in time, of Arthur's invasion of Poitou. Her grandson had joined forces at Tours with the Lusignan rebels and their men, who told him that the queen mother was travelling from Fontevrault to Poitiers, where she intended to take refuge. She would be a bargaining counter of unparalleled value, so—without waiting for the greater part of his troops, who were still on their way from Brittany, and against the advice of the French knights—the young duke led his little army to capture her. He learned that she had stopped with her small escort at the town of Mirebeau on the borders of Anjou and Poitou. He soon reached it and his men speedily stormed the walls.

The fierce old queen retreated into the small keep, probably scarcely more than a tower, which served as the town's citadel. She manned the ramparts with her few troops and refused to surrender, although there was only a thin wall between her and her grandson's men. Resourceful as ever, she then asked for a parley and began to bargain. Her besiegers did not know that she had secretly sent two messengers for help: one to William of Les Roches, the seneschal of Anjou, at Chinon, and one to king John at Le Mans. Unsuspectingly, Arthur's soldiers made no attempt to storm the keep but waited for Eleanor to surrender. They had barred all the gates in the town walls to prevent anyone escaping from the keep, but had left a single gate open in order to admit their own food.

As soon as the queen's messenger reached Le Mans, John started on the one gallant enterprise of his life. He came at once, covering eighty miles in forty-eight hours, riding through the night as well as the day. William of Les Roches and the garrison of Chinon joined him en route. They reached Mirebeau at dawn on 1 August. At the council of war just before the attack, William of Les Roches asked the king to promise to put none of his captives to death, to treat his nephew as though there was no war between them, and to confine Arthur's supporters in the immediate locality until a truce had been arranged. John agreed, telling William that he and the other lords present could refuse their homage and cease to recognize him as their king if he broke his word. Then the royal army attacked, pouring into Mirebeau through the open gate.

It was a hot night and, with no thought of danger, Arthur's men had not bothered to sleep in their armour. When Geoffrey of Lusignan was interrupted during a hearty breakfast of roast pigeon and told that the king of England was attacking, he laughed and said that he would finish his breakfast. There was a bloody scuffle in the narrow little streets of Mirebeau, but Arthur's troops had been caught in a trap from which there was no escape and they were hopelessly outnumbered. Their attackers quickly overpowered them.

Indeed king John had won an extraordinary victory in the only engagement in which he personally commanded his troops during his entire reign. Arthur had brought no more than 250 knights but these included the two most important members of the Lusignan clan, Hugh the Brown and his uncle Geoffrey. The king had captured not only Philip II's chief ally but the principal leaders of the revolt in Poitou. He had also captured Arthur's heiress, his unmarried sister Eleanor of Brittany, who had adventurously ridden with her brother. It was a dazzling success, and should have completely altered the course of the war. If Richard had still been king, Philip would almost certainly have hastened to make peace. As it was, he abandoned the siege of Arques and retreated, and John was able to capture both Angers and Tours. But the English king did not know how to use his victory.

Instead of keeping the promises he had made to William of Les Roches, John inflicted on his prisoners every humiliation he could think of. The noblest lords were packed 'as though they were calves' into ox carts and chained together, their faces to the beasts' tails as an added refinement, and dragged in triumph through their own domains; to ride in a cart was the ultimate disgrace for any knight. Hugh the Brown was confined in a prison in Normandy, but most of his companions were shipped to England to await ransom, where some are said to have been blinded. Probably at least twenty were deliberately starved to death at Corfe castle because they could not find the money to buy their freedom. But the one man whom the king should have kept in prison—Hugh the Brown, the leader of the Lusignan party—was allowed to ransom himself.

Beyond question, king John was fiendishly cruel and blood-thirsty. Quite apart from the prisoners of Corfe, he was to have all too many murders to his discredit. The barbarous mass-acre of 300 captives at Evreux has already been mentioned. There is little evidence for the popular tale that in order to make a Jew of Bristol disgorge his gold he tortured him by pulling out several teeth a day, but the story has the stamp of John's peculiar sense of humour. Half a dozen chroniclers bear witness to a much more horrifying crime. The wife of William of Braose—a once loyal supporter who eventually turned against the king—refused to hand over her children to John as hostages; when he caught Matilda of Braose, he deliberately starved her to death at Windsor with her elder son; their corpses were found after eleven days without food and it was seen that in her agony the mother had gnawed her own child's cheeks. John hanged twenty-eight Welsh boys who were hostages for their chieftain fathers' good behaviour. He also hanged a man and his son for prophesying (wrongly) the date when the king's reign would end. Many others met a violent death in his dungeons or simply disappeared.

In these circumstances, duke Arthur's prospects were bleak. All that is known for certain about Arthur after his capture is that he was imprisoned at Falaise, where his gaoler apparently treated him well enough. According to Roger of Wendover—frequently unreliable, but he may well have been telling the truth in this instance—the young duke spent some months in a dungeon at Falaise, and then the king came to see him. It seems that for once John was in a merciful mood, if Roger is to be believed. The king told his nephew that he would set him free and give him back his duchy of Brittany if he would break with Philip II and promise homage and loyalty. But the young duke was not a Plantagenet for nothing and appears to have possessed all his father's and his uncles' insane pride. Even after a long and miserable imprisonment he showed his evil streak. (In 1199, dis-cussing him with Hubert Walter, William Marshal had already discerned it.) Arthur answered fiercely that he would never make peace until he had obtained not merely Brittany but everything that had belonged to his uncle Richard, including the kingdom of England. John immediately ordered that Arthur should be moved to Rouen, where he was confined in a newly built tower, 'and not long after that, Arthur suddenly vanished'.

Nobody knows what happened. Ralph of Coggeshall, who took pains to be as accurate as possible about most matters, says that because the Bretons were in revolt over their duke's imprisonment 'the king's counsellors' had already suggested that Arthur should be blinded and castrated 'so that he would thereafter be incapable of princely rule'. Ralph further tells us that John had ordered Hubert de Burgh to do this, when Arthur was at Falaise, but that Hubert disobeyed him. (Ralph's version is very likely the origin of Shakespeare's scene, 'Heat me these irons hot'.) There was also a contemporary rumour, perhaps put about by the court, that Arthur had fallen from a high tower while trying to escape. A French life of Philip II, the *Philippide*, says that John took the boy out onto the Seine in a boat, where he cut his throat and threw him overboard.

The last story may contain an element of truth. Among the king's counsellors at this time, William of Braose was one of the most important, perhaps the most important of all. A benefactor of the Cistercian monastery of Margam in Wales, William may have confided the secret to its monks after he turned against John. Certainly the *Annals of Margan* contain an extremely plausible account: at Rouen on Maundy Thursday 1203 the king, 'when he was drunk and possessed by the devil' (*ebrius et daemonio plenus*), killed Arthur with his own hand and then dropped the corpse into the Seine after tying a heavy stone to it. A fisherman dredged up the body in his net and it was identified and secretly buried at a nearby Benedictine priory 'in fear of the tyrant'.

In 1203 Maundy Thursday fell on 3 April. Not quite a

fortnight later, on 16 April, king John sent a certain brother
John of Valerant to queen Eleanor with a letter. The king said
that God had been kind to him and that the messenger could tell
her all about it. It has been suggested that the king was referring
to the death of his nephew, with the inference that Eleanor may
even have welcomed the murder. This seems most unlikely, as
the letter was addressed to eight other people as well, including
the archbishop of Bordeaux.

The rightful duchess of Brittany was now Arthur's elder
sister, Eleanor, who had been taken prisoner with him at Mirebeau. Being unmarried, she constituted almost as much of a
danger to John as had Arthur. Indeed she was also the heiress of
the king himself, for the king was as yet childless. The fate of the
'pearl of Brittany' remained unknown for a long time: no doubt
many contemporaries suspected that she too had been murdered.
In fact she was merely taken to England and put in close confinement, apparently in some comfort; her uncle provided her with
money, expensive clothes and other luxuries. Nevertheless,
despite the pleas of the bishops of Brittany and the demands of
the king of France, John always refused to release her. At one
time it seems that he considered using her as a puppet duchess
of Brittany and she was taken to France on one of the king's
later campaigns, but the scheme came to nothing and she
remained in prison at various castles—mainly Bristol—until
she died, forty years after her capture. She was buried at the
Fontevrault priory of Amesbury. (There is a curious legend
that John's son, Henry III, felt so guilty about the cousin who
should have sat on his throne that he once presented her with
a gold crown, but that she gave it back to him after a few
days.)

One may well ask whether queen Eleanor must take any of
the blame for her grandson's murder. Certainly Arthur and his
mother had been her sworn enemies and he had tried to lay
hands on her at the point of the sword: still more unforgivably,

he had intended to take away her lands, power and independence. Knowing John, she must surely have foreseen what might happen to the wretched youth. Yet on the other hand, though plainly no friend to Arthur, it is quite likely that she thought he would simply remain in perpetual confinement, as in fact happened to his sister. One has to take into account the story that at one moment John actually thought of releasing Arthur. The most convincing testimony to Eleanor's innocence in this matter is her shrewdness. She was too far-sighted a politician not to realize that the young duke's murder would prove disastrous for her son's cause. Not only did it give his enemies moral justification for making war on king John, but it also enabled Philip of France to claim homage from Arthur's outraged vassals.

20 The End of the Angevin Empire

'What! mother dead?
How wildly then walks my estate in France!'
Shakespeare, *King John*

'Now boast thee, death! In thy possession lies
A lass unparallel'd.'
Shakespeare, *Antony and Cleopatra*

It can truly be said that the Angevin empire died with Eleanor of Aquitaine. In a sense it had only come into being because of her, and it passed with her, although it was no fault of her's that it came to an end: indeed it was the Norman and Plantagenet possessions that were lost, not Aquitaine. Perhaps she realized that her unbalanced youngest child would find it impossible to hold such a vast inheritance, and that Richard's death had spelt its doom. Yet, shrewd as she was, probably even the old queen found it hard to believe that Philip II was capable of conquering her sons' great fiefs in France. And while she lived, she could try to stave off disaster.

Nevertheless, one person considered that Eleanor was responsible for the coming débâcle, which he foresaw only too clearly. When the bishop of Lincoln, St Hugh, lay dying during the last months of 1200 he made a dismal prophecy:

> The descendants of king Henry must bear the curse pronounced in Holy Scripture: 'The multiplied brood of the wicked shall not thrive; and bastard slips shall not take deep root nor any fast foundation,' and again: 'The children of adulterers shall be rooted out.' The present king of France will avenge the memory of his virtuous father, king Louis, upon the children of the faithless wife who left him to unite with his enemy. And as the ox eats down the grass to the very roots, so shall Philip of France entirely destroy this race.

The early thirteenth century was accustomed to bloodshed but it is clear that contemporaries were genuinely shocked by the murder of Arthur, although they could only guess at what had happened. As late as October 1203 Philip II did not know whether the young duke was dead or alive, but he obviously had his suspicions. William of Les Roches, to whom John had sworn that Arthur should come to no harm, turned against the king of England, almost certainly from revulsion. William was a serious loss; he was not only one of the greatest lords in Anjou, and its seneschal, but also one of John's most capable commanders.

Many others of the English king's subjects were outraged, not least those in Brittany, where the young duke seems to have been extremely popular. Philip of France called upon John in the name of the Bretons to show that Arthur was still alive.

In any case Philip's troops were already invading Normandy, while a Breton army was attacking it from the south-west. The Norman border was quickly conquered and then strongholds in the heart of the duchy began to fall, some surrendering because John had not made proper provision for their defence, and others because they preferred to be ruled by king Philip. For the Normans were war weary, crushed by savage taxation and by the ravages of John's mercenaries. Furthermore the suspicious English king would not trust the Norman barons and set them against him by preferring to use his own paid henchmen.

King John wandered aimlessly through eastern Normandy, with his treasure and his hostages, apparently incapable of any proper plan for a defensive campaign. By the end of 1203 probably only the Cotentin, Mortain and Rouen remained loyal to him. Château-Gaillard was still holding out, although it had been besieged since August and an attempt to relieve it had failed. The king could do nothing but mutter helplessly, 'Let me alone!' as news of fresh enemy advances kept on coming in; 'One day I shall reconquer all I have lost'. At the beginning of December John gave way to despair and left Normandy for England, never to return.

In March 1204 Philip made sure of victory in Normandy, taking Château-Gaillard by assault. The greatest stronghold in France had fallen, although it was supposed to be impregnable. The French king struck westwards to join forces with the Bretons. Early in the summer Falaise, also thought impregnable, surrendered after a siege of only seven days, and then Caen and Bayeux went too. Avranches was taken by the Bretons. By the end of May only Rouen, the ducal capital, continued to hold out for John. Its garrison commander, Peter of Préaux, sent a desperate appeal to the king in England, but was told that he would have to help himself. Accordingly, on 24 June Rouen surrendered to Philip II. Save for the Channel Islands, king John had lost the entire Norman heritage bequeathed by his great-great-grandfather, William the Conqueror.

It was the first step down in a very gloomy descent indeed. John's reign became steadily more disastrous. His oppressive government and savagery alienated not just his vassals in France but the English baronage as well. He also made an enemy of the Church, which eventually excommunicated both king and kingdom. His road led to Runnymede and the humiliating concessions of Magna Carta. It ended in an invasion of England by Philip II's troops during which the country was nearly lost to the Plantagenets; a septuagenarian William Marshal saved the throne with difficulty for John's son, the boy king Henry III.

In the meantime William of Les Roches seized Angers and quickly won control of all Anjou. In August 1204, in his capacity of seneschal, he surrendered the county to Philip. By 1205 Maine and Touraine, together with the north and east of Poitou, had gone the same way.

In Poitou, however, there had been some genuine resistance to Philip. Eleanor had a loyal and efficient commander in the seneschal, Robert of Thornham. Moreover, Philip was to some extent deterred by the fact that in theory he had no legal quarrel with Eleanor, who had done homage to him as his vassal. One may guess, too, that the defence was stiffened by the indomitable old lady. She had now moved from Fontevrault to Poitiers; after her unpleasant experience at Mirebeau she had been forced to stay in the safety of the capital, since the entire county was torn by war. Even Eleanor could not stop the rot in her own territory. The Lusignan party had become too deeply entrenched, and too many of the other Poitevin lords had been outraged by John's behaviour. She was too old and frail to lead a full-scale campaign against them. Nevertheless she still had just enough strength to try to keep the county loyal, although well over eighty and obviously failing. As late as 1203 she wooed the citizens of Niort by granting them a charter.

John did nothing to help her. Some historians have attempted to show that he tried to halt the Capetian invasion, but a contemporary troubadour tells a very different story. Writing apparently at the beginning of 1205 Bertran de Born's son composed a *sirventès* (or satirical ballad) 'to make king John blush for shame'. It seems that he did so at the request of one of John's most loyal officers, Savary de Mauléon. The troubadour says that the king ought to be ashamed to think of his ancestors after having abandoned Poitou to Philip II 'for the asking', and that all Aquitaine regrets *lo rei Richart*, whom his brother is so plainly incapable of emulating. The younger Bertran adds sarcastically that one can scarcely compare John to Sir Gawain (the Arthurian hero), and that the king prefers hunting or sheer idleness to anything else, which is why he has lost both his honour and his lands. The poem ends by calling John a flabby coward who does not know how to fight and can inspire loyalty in no one.

No doubt the queen mother felt increasingly that her own end was near, when she heard almost every day how some fresh disaster had befallen her son. It has been suggested that the news of the loss of Château-Gaillard—Richard's creation—killed her. There are varying accounts of her last days, but it seems most likely that she left the security of Poitiers and returned to her dear Fontevrault. Here, apparently, she died as she must have hoped, wearing the black-and-white habit of its nuns. This was on either 31 March or 1 April 1204. She was buried in the crypt of the abbey church. On 10 August 1204 Philip II rode into Poitiers and took possession of the Maubergeon.

Shakespeare was probably correct in guessing that king John regarded his mother's death as the final ruin of all his hopes in France. In the words of bishop Stubbs, Eleanor was 'the great source and prop of his continental position. . . . John's fortunes are not wholly hopeless until he loses his mother'. Even when she was too aged to be of any active assistance, she must still have had considerable value as a focus of loyalty and a symbol of strength. She could have been yet more useful as an adviser, although the king was probably too stupid to ask her advice, as he demonstrated by his murder of Arthur. Indeed apart from their dramatic meeting at Mirebeau there is little evidence that he saw anything of his mother during her final years. It was therefore fitting that he should not be present at her deathbed. She had never felt much love for him, nor had she ever been tolerant of failure, and certainly she had never known failure on such a grand scale as that of John. Out of all the Angevin empire in France, only Aquitaine remained, except for a strip of southwestern Poitou. Admittedly Aquitaine may have had little wish to be ruled by a northern Frenchman such as king Philip II. Yet it is conceivable that the Aquitainians preferred to stay loyal to John simply because he was the son of their magnificent duchess.

Was Eleanor another empress Livia or was she the 'woman beyond compare' of Richard of Devizes? The most important hostile testimony is that of St Hugh of Lincoln, whose prophecy of the imminent end of the Plantagenet dynasty all but came true. This Carthusian bishop was not just an eccentric clairvoyant. On the contrary, he was a very practical saint who despised popularity, protected Jews, and defied in turn Henry II, Richard I and John—each of whom respected and liked him, even John. Far from being a misogynist like St Bernard, Hugh thoroughly enjoyed having pious ladies to dine with him. Yet Hugh regarded Eleanor as a wicked adulteress whose sin had left an appalling curse on her progeny, although in the same breath he could speak in the warmest terms of Louis VII, the husband who had cast her off. It is difficult to explain this apparent confusion in the saint's mind. Perhaps he believed, mistakenly, that Louis had repudiated his queen because of adultery. A more sinister interpretation of his condemnation is that he thought he recognized some inherent evil in Eleanor.

It is reassuring that other contemporaries had a different opinion of her. Half a century later the chronicler Matthew Paris wrote of 1204, 'In this year the noble queen Eleanor, a woman of admirable beauty and intelligence, died'. And Matthew had surely spoken with people who remembered her. As for her virtues, the good sisters of Fontevrault—who admittedly must have been somewhat biased—extolled their benefactress in their necrology, claiming that 'in the conduct of her blameless life, she surpassed all the queens of the world'. No doubt they were thinking of the devout old lady whom they had known when she had spent her last years with them, not of the mother queen who, in her lust for power, had raised a vast international rebellion against her husband and turned his own children against him, who had made almost a lover out of her favourite son, and who had ruthlessly altered the succession to the Angevin empire. The nuns conveniently forgot the frivolous patroness of troubadours who had dared to laugh at St Bernard and the monks, the haughty, luxury-loving queen who had ridden in pomp through so many exotic capitals and who had even threatened a pope. All that was many years ago and the nuns may be forgiven; her life, though hardly a happy one, had been so long and varied that it was impossible for ordinary mortals to understand her, let alone to judge her. Certainly Eleanor's love of Fontevrault and the years that she spent there are the best witness in her defence.

Eleanor of Aquitaine will always remain a fascinating enigma. Her elegant effigy still lies gracefully at Fontevrault, crowned and wimpled and holding a prayer book. She is between her estranged husband Henry II, who stole her inheritance and imprisoned her, and that dearest of all sons, Richard Coeur-de-lion. Nearby lie her daughter Joanna of Toulouse and her daughter-in-law Isabella of Angoulême. By the conventions of mediaeval art her marble face can scarcely be a natural likeness, but it is the face of an extraordinarily attractive woman.

Select Bibliography

CONTEMPORARY SOURCES

Adam of Eynsham, *The Life of St Hugh of Lincoln*, edited and translated by D.L. Douie and H. Fanner, Nelson, 1961–2

Audiau, J. (editor), *Nouvelle Anthologie des Troubadours*, Paris, 1928

Benedict of Peterborough, *Gesta Regis Henrici Secundi*, edited by W. Stubbs, Rolls Series, 1867

Benedict of Sainte Maure, *Chronique des ducs de Normandie*, edited by F. Michel, Paris, 1938

Bernard of Clairvaux, *Oeuvres completes De Saint Bernard*, Paris, 1873

Garmonsway, G.N. (editor and translator), *The Anglo-Saxon Chronicle*, J.M. Dent, 1953

Geoffrey of Monmouth, *Historia regum Britanniae*, edited and translated by A. Griscom and R. E. Jones, New York, 1929

Geoffrey of Vigé, *La Chronique de Geoffroy, Prieur de Vigeois*, edited and translated by F. Bonnélye, Tulle, 1864

Gerald of Wales (Giraldus Cambrensis), *Opera*, edited by J. S. Brewer, J. F. Dimock, and G. F. Warner, Rolls Series, 1861–91

—, *The Autobiography of Gerald the Welshman*, translated by H. E. Butler, Jonathan Cape, 1937

—, *The First Version of the Topography of Ireland by Giraldus Cambrensis*, translated by J.J. O'Meara, Dundalk, 1951

—, *Concerning the Instruction of Princes*, translated by J. Stevenson, London, 1858

Gervase of Canterbury, *The Historical Works*, edited by W. Stubbs, Rolls Series, 1879–80

Henry of Huntingdon, *Historia Anglorum*, edited by T. Arnold, Rolls Series 1879

John of Salisbury, *The Letters of John of Salisbury*, edited and translated by W.J. Miller and C.N.L. Brooke, Nelson, 1955

—, *Memoirs of the Papal Court*, edited by M. Chibnall, Nelson, 1956

257

Margam, *Annales de Margan*, edited by H. R. Luard, Rolls Series, 1864

Matthew Paris, *Historia Minor*, edited by Sir F. Madden, Rolls Series, 1866–9

Meyer, P. (editor and translator), *Histoire de Guillaume le Maréchal*, Paris, 1891–1901

Odo of Deuil, *De Profectione Ludovici VII in Orientem*, edited by H. Waquet, Paris, 1949

Ordericus Vitalis, *The Ecclesiastical History of England and Normandy*, edited by T. Forester, London, 1853

Peter of Blois, *Opera Omnia*, edited by J. P. Migne in *Patrologiae Cursus Completus* (series Latina, vol. CCVII), Paris, 1855

Ralph of Coggeshall, *Chronicon Anglicanum* edited by J. Stevenson, Rolls Series, 1875

Ralph of Diceto, *Opera Historica*, edited by W. Stubbs, Rolls Series, 1876

Raynouard, F.J.M. (editor), *Choix des poésies originales des troubadours*, Paris, 1816–21

Richard of Devizes, *Chronicle*, edited by J. T. Appleby, Nelson's Mediaeval Texts, 1963

Richard FitzNigel, *Dialogus de Scaccario*, edited by C. Johnson, Nelson's Mediaeval Texts, 1963

Rigord, *Gesta Philippi Augusti*, edited by H. F. Delaborde, Paris, 1882

Robert of Torigny, *Chronica Roberti de Torigneio* in *Chronicles of the Reigns of Stephen, Henry II and Richard I*, edited by R. Hewlett, Rolls Series, 1884–9

Roger of Howden, *Chronica*, edited by W. Stubbs, Rolls Series, 1868–71

Roger of Wendover, *Flores Historiarum*, edited by H. G. Hewlett, Rolls Series, 1886–9

Suger, *Historia Ludovici VII*, edited by A. Molinier, Paris, 1887

William of Malmesbury, *De Regum Gestis Anglorum*, edited by W. Stubbs, Rolls Series, 1887–9

William of Newburgh, *Historia Rerum Anglicarum* in *Chronicles of the Reigns of Stephen, Henry II and Richard I*, edited by R. Hewlett, Rolls Series, 1884–9

William of Poitiers, *Les Chansons de Guillaume IX, duc d'Aquitaine*, edited by A. Jeanroy, Paris, 1927

William of Tyre, *A History of Deeds done beyond the Sea*, translated by E. A. Babcock and A. C. Krey, New York, 1943

Select Bibliography

SECONDARY SOURCES

Bezzola, R. *Les origines et la formation de la littérature courtoise en occident (500–1200)*, Paris, 1958–63

Boissonade, P. *Histoire de Poitou*, Paris, 1926

Chaytor, H.J. *The Troubadours*, CUP, 1912

Cockayne, G.E. and Gibbs, V. (editors), *The Complete Peerage*, St Catherine's Press, 1910–59

Dictionary of National Biography

Dictionnaire de Biographie Française, Paris, 1933–67

Fawtier, R. *The Capetian Kings of France*, translated by L. Butler and R.J. Adam, Macmillan, 1960

Grousset, R. *Histoire des Croisades et du Royaume Franc de Jérusalem*, Paris, 1934–6

Kelly, A. *Eleanor of Aquitaine and the Four Kings*, Cassell, 1952

Knowles, Dom D. *Thomas Becket*, A. & C. Black, 1971

——, *The Episcopal Colleagues of Thomas Becket*, CUP, 1961

Labande, E.R. *Pour une image véridique d'Aliénor d'Aquitaine* in *Bulletin de la Société des Antiquaires de l'Ouest*, 4 série, ii, Poitiers, 1952

Norgate, K. *England under the Angevin Kings*, London, 1887

——, *Richard the Lion Heart*, London 1924

——, *John Lackland*, New York, 1902

Painter, S. *The Reign of King John*, Baltimore, 1949

Paqaut, M. *Louis VII et son royaume*, Paris, 1964

Pernoud, R. *Aliénor d'Aquitaine*, Paris, 1965

Poole, A. L. *From Domesday Book to Magna Carta, 1087–1216*, OUP, 1951

Powicke, Sir M. *The Loss of Normandy, 1189–1203*, Manchester, 1961

Richardson, H. G. *The Letters and Charters of Eleanor of Aquitaine* in *English Historical Review* vol lxxiv, 1959

Rosenberg, M. V. *Eleanor of Aquitaine*, New York, 1937

Runciman, Sir S. *A History of the Crusades*, CUP, 1951–4

Salvini, J. *Aliénor d'Aquitaine* in *Dictionnaire de Biographie Française*

Stenton, F. M. *Norman London, an Essay* (with a translation of William FitzStephen's description by H. E. Butler), Historical Association Leaflets, 1934

Strickland, A. *Eleanor of Aquitaine* in *The Lives of the Queens of England*, London, 1840–8

Stubbs, W. *The Early Plantagenets*, London, 1903

——, *The Constitutional History of England*, OUP, 1883
Waddell, H. *The Wandering Scholars*, Pelican, 1954
Warren, W.L. *King John*, Eyre & Spottiswoode, 1962
——, *Henry II*, Eyre Methuen, 1974
Webb, G. *Fontevrault* in *Life of the Spirit*, January, 1962

Index

Abelard, Peter, 28, 32, 61
Acre, 52, 160, 168
Adelaide of Savoy, 30
Adela of Champagne, 100
Adrian IV, 121
Aélith (Petronilla), 18, 32, 36
Aénor of Châtellerault, 13, 18
Agnes of Meran, queen of France, 209
Alaiz of Ventadour, 73
Albigensians, 19, 20
Alexander III, 120
Alfonso II of Aragon, 114
Alfonso VIII of Castile, 120, 129, 233
Alice of Antioch, 49
Alice of Blois, 58, 114
Alice of France, 118, 139, 145, 156-9,
   167, 173, 191
Amaury of Thouars, 226, 237
Amesbury priory, 247
Anacletus, 18
Angers, 73, 147, 222-3, 244, 253
Angevin empire, lineage, 90; under
   Henry, 93, 99, 117, 129, 143, 146;
   under John, 219, 223-4, 228, 231;
   under Richard, 165, 193, 210;
   decline of, 103, 242, 251, 255
Angoulême, 139
Angoulême, count of, 109, 131, 235-6
Angoulême, Isabella of, 235-6, 241,
   256
Anjou, 69, 71, 117, 131, 146, 167,
   223-6, 228, 242-3, 251, 253
Antioch, 47-8
Antwerp, 180
Aquitaine, duchy of, geography, 13-14;
   Otto as duke, 193, 210; under Henry,
   70, 71, 93, 97-8, 100, 109, 114, 118,
   127-8, 131; under John, 219-20,
   224-5, 251, 255; under Louis, 20, 21,
   31, 58, 61-3; under Richard, 139,
   143, 167, 190, 207
Aragon, 16
Aragon, queen of, 96
Architecture, 14, 27-8, 34, 86, 178, 204
Arques, 59, 242, 244
Arthur, duke of Brittany, 144; as heir
   presumptive, 159, 165, 192-3, 219-
   20, 235; fighting John, 223-7; death
   of, 242-8, 251-2, 255
Arthurian literature, 74, 88, 111
Aumâle, 208, 242
Austria, duke Leopold of, 169-70, 174,
   178
Austria, Ida of, 42
Auvergne, 191, 228
Avranches, 129, 252

Baldwin, archbishop of Canterbury,
   143, 152
Baldwin III of Jerusalem, 52
Balun, 226
Barcelona, count of, 99

Basques, 13
Bath, bishop of, 172
Bayeux, 101, 189, 252
Becket, St Thomas, 28, 87, 95-100,
   101-2, 120, 129
Beauvain, Philip of Dreux, bishop of,
   208-9
Belin, 13, 19
Benedictines, 87, 198, 246
Berengaria, 158, 160-1, 169, 188, 193,
   213, 220, 225
Bernard, see St Bernard
Bernart de Ventadour, 73, 110
Berry, 146, 228
Bertha of Sulzbach, 45
Bertrada of Montfort, 201
Bertran de Born, 110, 112-3, 122-3,
   140-1, 254
Berwick, 155
Blachernae Palace, 44
Blanca of Castile, 233-4
Blois, count of, 33, 120, 131, 231
Brabançons, 208, 223
Brehon law, 121
Brie, count of, 33
Bristol, 72, 247
Brittany, 98, 103, 119, 124, 128, 131-
   2, 167, 228, 242, 245-7, see also
   Arthur of, Conan of, Constance of,
   Eleanor of, Geoffrey of
Brittany, bishop of, 247
Bohemond II, 49
Bonneville-sur-Touques, 167
Bordeaux, 13, 22, 224, 234
Bordeaux, archbishop of, 234, 247
Boulogne, Eustace of, 71
Bourges, 13, 27. 41
Boxley, abbot of, 172
Bures, 114, 120
Bury St Edmunds, 93, 188

Cadurc, 32
Caen, 189, 252
Cahors, 99
Canterbury, 120, 187
Capetian dynasty, under Louis VI,
   20-1; under Louis VII, 31, 58, 61,
   63, 71, 129; under Philip II, 146,
   207, 210, 234, 254
Carthusians, 28, 255
Castile, 231, 233
Castile, Alfonso VIII of, 120, 129
Celestine II, 35
Celestine III, 160, 172-4, 188
Cercamon, 17, 36
Champagne, 33-6, 57, 231, see also
   Adela of, Henry of, Marie of, and
   Thibault of
Channel Islands, 253
Chartres, bishop of, 22
Château-Gaillard, 207, 209-10, 252,
   254

Index

Chester, earl of, 131
Chinon, 114, 130, 133, 147, 151, 157, 197, 222, 226, 243
Chrétien de Troyes, 88, 110
Cistercians, 28, 33, 121, 246
Clairvaux, 18
Clarendon, 86
Cluny, 87
Cologne, 180, 209
Compostella, 21
Conan IV, duke of Brittany, 103, 119
Conrad III of Germany, 41-2, 44, 46, 52
Constance of Antioch, 49
Constance of Brittany, 103, 144, 192, 219-20, 222-3, 226, 228
Constance of Castile, 97
Constance of France, 99
Constantinople, 44-5, 93
Corbeil, 33
Corfe castle, 244-5
Corfu, 169
Cotentin, 252
crossbow, 208
Crusades, 15, 42, 45, 47, 139, 145-6, 155-6, 176
Cyprus, 161, 169

Dangerosa of Châtellerault, 16, 17
Denmark, Ingeborg of, 209
Derby, earl of, 131
Dieppe, 191, 242
Dover Castle, 166
Drincourt, 241
Dublin, 121
Durham, bishop of, 188
Dürnstein, 170, 172

Edessa, 41, 51
Elbe II of Ventadour, 73
Eleanor of Aquitaine, 13, 18, 20, 49, 64, 69; Becket and, 95-6, 102; character, 17, 20, 22, 75, 109-10, 154, 197, 256; children, 35-6, 58, 62-4, 73, 89-90, 95, 98, 103, 107, 118, 120, 141, 191-4, 231-2; church and, 89, 141, 197ff, 256; court, influence on, 28, 45, 48ff, 110ff; crusader, 41ff; death, 251-4; education, 15, 19, 29; governing, 85, 93, 152, 165ff; Henry II and, 60, 69-70, 79, 88, 93-5, 97, 107, 137, 143; imprisonment, 138ff; John and, 193, 220, 222, 224-5; Louis VII and, 21-3, 27, 29-30, 36, 42, 50-3, 57ff; plot against Henry II, 107, 109, 114, 117-19, 122, 124, 127ff; Richard and, 118, 173, 187ff, 211-14; St Bernard and, 35, 61, 64
Eleanor of Brittany, 178, 244, 247
Eleanor of Castile, 89, 101, 120, 129, 231
Ermengarde of Narbonne, 74, 114
Etampes, 43
Eu, county of, 241
Eudo de Porhoet, 119
Eugenius III, 41, 43, 57-8, 64
Eustace of Boulogne, 71
Everswell, 88
Evreux, 190, 223, 228, 245
Eye, honour of, 190

Falaise, 245-6, 252
fashion, 28-9, 34-5, 45, 79, 113
Faye-la-Vineuse, 132-3
Ferrers of Derby, earl, 72, 87
feudal law, 13, 20, 210, 219, 224, 242
Flanders, 191

Flanders, count of, 131, 207
Flanders, countess of, 114
Fontainebleau, 167, 241
Fontevrault, 28, 43, 137-8, 151, 157, 197-204, 211, 213-14, 234, 237, 242, 253-4, 256
Fornham, 131
Frederick Barbarossa, 129
Frederick II, emperor, 209
Fulk of Nerra, 90
Fulk of Jerusalem, 49
Fulk of Neuilly, 193

Ganina, 170
Gascony, 13
Gaucelm Faidit, 110, 213
Genoa, 157
Geoffrey, archbishop of Loroux, 22
Geoffrey of Brittany, 89, 103, 119, 123-4, 131-2, 144, 192
Geoffrey of Lusignan, 236, 243, 244
Geoffrey Plantagenet, count of Anjou, 59-60, 71
Geoffrey Plantagenet of York, 107, 147, 155, 160, 166, 222
Geoffrey, son of Geoffrey of Anjou, 71-2
Germany, 29, 41, 172
Gilbert Foliot, bishop of Hereford, 87
Gisors, 132, 157, 167, 173, 208
Glastonbury, 89
Gloucester, 190
Gloucester, Isabella of, 155, 234-5
Godstow, 138
Gortz, Mainard, count of, 170
Gournai, 241
Grandmont, St Stephen of, 144
Greece, 45
Guienne, 13
Guy of Lusignan, 146
Guy of Thouars, 222

Hagenau, 175
Hainault, count of, 207
Hauteville dynasty, 158
Henry, duke of Saxony, 120, 231
Henry of Champagne, 169
Henry Plantagenet, 'The young king', 89, 98, 100, 117, 122, 127, 130, 132, 140-1, 213
Henry I, king of England, 20, 80-1, 201
Henry II, king of England, 59, 107, 227, 256; Becket and, 95-7, 120, 137; inheritance, 69-70, 75; king of England, 79ff, 121-2, 128-9, 131, 141ff, 147, see also Eleanor of Aquitaine, Henry II and, and plot
Henry III, king of England, 247, 253
Henry V, emperor, 20
Henry VI, of Hohenstaufen, emperor, 158, 170, 178-80, 190
Heraclea, 15
Heraclius, 146
Holy Land, 41, 48, 52, 139, 145, 155, 159, 168, 190
Hubert de Burgh, 246
Hubert Walter, 171-2, 175, 178, 188, 219, 226-7, 245
Hugh Bigod, earl of Norfolk, 72, 87
Hugh of Lincoln, see St Hugh
Hugh Puisset, bishop of Durham, 154, 156
Hugh IX (the Brown) of Lusignan, 233, 235-6, 244
Humbert of Maurienne, 129
Hyacinth Bobo, 160

262

Index

Ida of Austria, 42
Ingeborg of Denmark, 209
Innocent II, 18, 32
Innocent III, 209, 225, 228, 235
Ireland, 120, 144, 190
Irene, empress of Greece, 45
Isaac Comnenus, 161
Isabella of Angoulême, 235-6, 241, 256
Isabella of Gloucester, 155, 234-5
Issoudun, 191

Jaffa, 168
Jerusalem, 42, 51-2, 145, 168, 231
Jews, 31, 61, 153, 156, 255
Joanna of Sicily, 89, 120, 139, 158, 160, 168, 169, 191-2, 203, 231, 256
John, king of England, 89, 107, 203, 211; campaign for throne, 165-7, 169, 171, 173-4, 176-7, 179, 188, 193; character, 147, 189-90, 192, 220-1; inheritance, 119, 129-30, 132, 142, 144-5, 155, 190; king of England, 219ff, 237, 241-4, 151-3, 255
John of Alencon, 189
John of Salisbury, 50, 57, 87, 89
John of Valerant, 247

Kent, 131
Knights Hospitallers, 157
Knights Templar, 47, 225

La Marche, 109, 233, 235-6, 241
La Maubergeonne, 16
language, 14, 80, 153
La Rochelle, 14, 224
Le Goulet, 228
Leicester, Robert Beaumont, earl of, 86, 131-2, 152, 173
Le Mans, 147, 223, 225-6, 242-3
Léon, king of, 233
Leopold, duke of Austria, 170, 174, 178
Le Perrot, 157
Lezay, 31
Limoges, 21, 63, 72, 114, 119, 210
Limoges, count of, 236
Lincoln, 93
literature, 14, 16, 28, 74, 88-9, 111
London, 79-80, 168, 187, 224
Louis VI, 20, 21, 23
Louis VII, character, 21, 29, 30-2, 90; church and, 21, 32-4, 120, 139, 255; crusader, 41ff; death, 140; Eleanor and, 21-3, 27, 29-30, 36, 42, 50-3, 57ff; king of France, 21, 71, 99-100, 103, 128, 130-2; marriages, 97, 100, 103
Louis VIII, 228
Louis IX, St Louis, 231, 234
Louvain, duke of, 180
Low Countries, 180
Lusignans, 109, 131, 233, 235, 237, 241-2, 253

Magna Carta, 253
Mainard, count of Gortz, 170
Maine, 68, 117, 128, 131, 146, 193, 219, 223-6, 228, 253
Malcolm IV, king of Scotland, 99, 101
Manichaeism, 19, 192
Manuel Comnenus, 44
Marcabru, 36, 43
Margam abbey, 246
Margaret, daughter to Louis VII, 98, 100, 117, 123, 129

Marie of Champagne, 36, 110, 113, 225
Marie of France, 88, 110
Marseilles, 157
Matilda of Braose, 245
Matilda, duchess of Saxony, 89, 120, 142, 193, 232
Matilda, empress of Germany, 74, 93, 109, 127
Matilda of Anjou, abbess of Fontevrault, 201, 211
Maubergeon, 16, 19, 110, 254
Mercadier, 208, 211, 233-4
Messina, 157
Metz, 43
Mirebeau, 130, 243-4, 247, 253, 255
Montmirail, 117-18, 129
Montmorency, lord of, 30
Montreuil-Bellay, Rigaud Berlai, lord of, 59
Mortain, 165, 190, 252

Nantes, 98
Niort, 119, 224, 254
Norfolk, earl of, 131
Normandy, claims on, 117, 143, 242; under Henry II, 59, 100, 131; under John, 223-5, 234-7, 241, 244, 251-2; under Richard, 167, 177, 188-9, 207, 211
Northampton, 102
Nottingham, 188
Noyon, bishop of, 32

Odo of Deuil, 44, 47
Old king, see Henry II
Old Sarum, 137-8, 142
Ombrière Palace, 19, 22
Orford Castle, 178
Orleans, 13, 28
Otto IV (of Brunswick), emperor, 193, 210, 222, 228
Oxford, 74, 168
Oxford, archdeacon of, 171

Palermo, 52
Paris, 13, 27, 130-1, 224, 241
Patrick, earl of Salisbury, 87, 110
Penthièvre, 119
Peter of Blois, archbishop of Bath and London, 85, 172
Peter of Capua, 209
Peter of Préaux, 252
Petronilla, (Aélith), 18, 32, 36
Philip of Dreux, bishop of Beauvain, 208-9
Philip II, king of France, 103, 139-40, 145-6; character, 207-9; enemy of John, 223, 226-7, 237, 241, 244-55; enemy of Richard, 165, 169-71, 173, 175, 177, 179, 189-90, 194, 207-8, 210-11, 219; on crusade, 157, 159, 167
Piedmont, 129
Pierre of le Châtre, 32-3, 36
Poitevins, 90, 140, 153, 214, 253
Poitiers, 13, 14, 22, 27, 31, 118, 224, 253-4
Poitiers, count of, 119
Poitou, 14, 71, 114, 131-2, 141, 144, 146, 167, 188, 219-20, 224-5, 235-6, 241-4, 253-5
Portsmouth, 189
Portugal, 235
Premonstratensians, 28

queen's gold, 93, 225

Index

Quercy, 99

Ralph, count of Eu, 236
Ralph of Coggeshall, 246
Ralph of Diceto, 13, 128, 151, 187
Ranuff, earl of Chester, 192
Ranulf de Glanvill, 138, 152, 171
Raoul, count of Vermandois, 22, 32
Raoul of Faye, 132
Raoul of Lusignan, 241
Raoul of Mauléon, 224
Raymond of Antioch, 49, 53
Raymond V of Toulouse, 99, 130, 146
Raymond VI of Toulouse, 191, 192, 203, 231
Raymond VII of Toulouse, 203
Renaissance, 28
Rhys of Dehoubarth, 101
Richard de Lucy, 86
Richard the Poitevin, 139
Richard I, king of England, 89, 95, 142-3, 210, 255; Alice of France and, 139, 145, 157; Berengaria and, 158-61, 193; capture in Germany, 169-80, 226; character, 123, 153, 189-90, 193-4, 213; crusader, 157-69; death, 203, 211, 213, 251; duke of Aquitaine, 139-40, 190-1; Eleanor and, 118, 151, 173, 187ff, 211-14, 256; Henry II and, 131-2, 139, 143, 144, 151; king of England, 151, 153, 188, 219, 227
Richeut Longchamp, 166
Rigaud Berlai, 59
Rigaut de Barbezieux, 110
Robert Beaumont, earl of Leicester, 72, 86, 152
Robert of Thornham, 225, 253
Robertsbridge, abbot of, 172
Roger, king of Sicily, 52
Rome, 58, 160
Rosamund Clifford, 107ff, 138
Rotrou of Warwick, 132
Rouen, 84, 95, 132, 144, 157, 161, 173, 191, 197, 207, 213, 224, 246, 252, 253
Rouen, archbishop of, 171, (see also Walter of Coutances)
Roxburgh, 155
Runnymede, 253

St Bernard, abbot of Clairvaux, 18, 32-4, 41, 57, 59-64, 201, 255-6
Saintes, 224
St Hugh of Lincoln, 17, 138, 166, 214, 220, 251, 255
St Paul's Cathedral, 176, 187
Saladin, 145, 168
Salisbury, 86, 171
Salisbury, earl of, 131
Samson, abbot of Bury St Edmunds, 176
Sancho VI of Navarre, 114, 158
Sancho of Portugal, 235
Sandwich, 183, 187
Saphadin, 168
Saracens, 15, 46, 51
Savary de Mauléon, 254
Savoy, 129
Saxony, duke of, 231
Shaftesbury, abbess of, 88
Sicily, 157, 179, 209, 231
Sirventès, 14, 254
Southampton, 75, 167
Speier, 42, 174, 179
Stephen of Blois, king of England, 29, 60, 71, 74, 81, 87

Stephen of Turnham, 183
Suger, abbot of St Denis, 21-2, 30, 36, 41, 43, 51-2, 58, 71

Talmont, 18-19, 31, 224
Tancred of Sicily, 158, 170, 175, 178
Theobald, archbishop of Canterbury, 79, 87, 98
Thibault II of Champagne, 22, 32-3, 36
Thierry Galeran, 51, 58, 63
Tickhill, 188
Toledo, 233
Toulouse, 15-16, 19, 31, 98-9, 129, 146, 191-2, 207
Touraine, 69, 146, 177, 190, 223, 226, 242, 253
Tours, 223-4, 242, 244
Troubadours, 14-15, 19, 28, 36, 43, 73, 110, 153, 202, 214
Trouvères, 28
Turks, 46, 48
Tusculum, 57

Uguccione Pierlone of Sant'Angelo, 137
Urraca, princess of Castile, 233

Vexin, 59, 98, 100, 145, 173, 191, 208, 248
Vézelay, 41, 157
Vienna, 169
Vitry (le Brûlé, en Perthois), 33, 41, 58

Wace of Jersey, 88
Wales, 101
Wallingford, 173-4
Walter de Clifford, 107
Walter Map, 29, 82
Walter of Coutances, 160, 167, 171, 178
Welf, 170, 174
Westminster, 82, 86, 96
Westminster Abbey, 117, 152
William Aigret, 18
William Atheling, 201
William Cade, 117
William Fitzstephen, 96, 138
William Longchamp, 154-6, 160, 165-7, 171, 175, 177-8, 226
William Longsword, earl of Salisbury, 107
William Marshal, 122, 147, 151, 154,, 219-20, 223, 227, 245, 253
William of Braose, 219, 245, 246
William of Les Roches, 223, 226, 243, 244, 251
William of Newburgh, 60, 82, 107, 176, 187, 235
William of Ponthieu, 191
William of Wareone, earl of Surrey, 87
William the Lion, king of Scotland, 132, 155
William the Conqueror, 253
William II of Sicily, 120, 139, 158
William IX, duke of Aquitaine, 13-17, 90, 201-2
William X, duke of Aquitaine, 13, 17, 18, 21
Winchester, 137-8, 142, 151, 152, 167, 189
Windsor, 142, 152, 167, 173, 174, 177, 245
women, status of, 14-15, 28, 34-5, 42, 44, 197, 201
Woodstock, 86, 88, 101, 108

York, 155, 171
young king, see Henry Plantagenet